Under Three Flags

Under Three Flags

Raymond Beecher

Raymond Beecher (signature)

BLACK · DOME

Black Dome Press Corp.
RR1, Box 422
Hensonville, NY 12439
Tel: (518)734-6357
Fax: (518)734-5802

First Edition, 1991
Published by Black Dome Press Corp.
RR1, Box 422
Hensonville, NY 12439
Tel: (518)734-6357
Fax: (518)734-5802

Library of Congress Catalog Card Number: 91-076679

ISBN 0-9628523-2-5

Cover design by Artemisia, Inc., Windham, NY

Printed in the USA

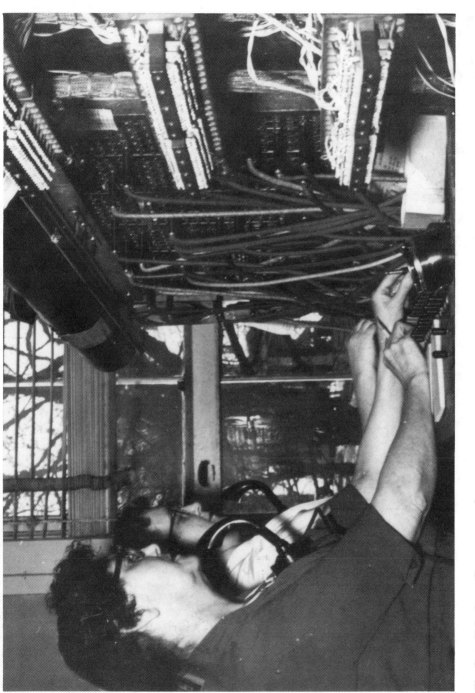

The State Telephone Company workers.
Courtesy of the State Telephone Company, Coxsackie, NY, a generous supporter of this edition.

The National Bank of Coxsackie. *Courtesy of the National Bank of Coxsackie, Coxsackie, NY, a generous supporter of this edition.*

 Contents

 Introduction

Founded on the west bank of the Hudson River, 125 miles from New York City, the Township of Coxsackie played a pivotal role in early American history. Originally a frontier outpost and trading port, the flat, fertile bottomland quickly attracted pioneers in business and agriculture. Among early settlements, the Pieter Bronck (whose family's New York City property later became known as "The Bronx") homestead is preserved today as the headquarters, museum and library of the Greene County Historical Society. Prominent resident, Leonard Bronk (surname spelling changed over the years) was a key figure in the Revolutionary War.

A scant twenty miles from the New York State capital at Albany, today's residential profile is a mix of rural farms, local service industry and Albany suburb. Coxsackie Township continues to experience change in its economic and social composition as it moves from a semirural to a semiurban environment.

In size, the Township covers approximately 38.75 square miles, extending in an easterly direction seven and three quarters miles, and running north-south for about five miles. In addition to the incorporated Village of Coxsackie (1867), the Township includes the hamlets of Climax and Earlton (Urlton). A 1990 population statistic of 7,403 persons, including New York State prison inmate population, indicates a 23 percent growth in the last decade.

Until the Act of the State Legislature, passed March 25, 1800, established the County of Greene, Coxsackie was one of several divisions of Albany County, the latter one of the political units of the Province and later the State of New York. Recognition of Coxsackie's population growth and importance came as early as July 3, 1718, when together with Catskill, it was designated a Precinct having its own justice of the peace and constable. At the same time it was authorized to elect a supervisor to represent its inhabitants on the Albany County Board.

Throughout these pre-Revolutionary eras of the eighteenth century, the settled areas of the Province of New York continued to expand along the Hudson Valley. This Anglo-Dutch population growth included the Precinct of Coxsackie and led to the Colonial Assembly, in 1772, designating Coxsackie a separate and distinct political entity—a District. Officials to be entrusted with its affairs included a supervisor, two assessors, a tax collector, two overseers of the poor, two constables, two fence viewers and a clerk. Like all other such existing districts in the State, by law passed March 7, 1788, Coxsackie was designated a township. Subsequently, as its undeveloped lands were settled, additional townships were set off from Coxsackie: Freehold (the western territory) in 1790, a part of Cairo (Canton) and Greenville (Greenfield) in 1803, and New Baltimore in 1811. Finally, in 1815, its most southerly section was incorporated into the newly established Township of Athens.

Greene County, of which Coxsackie Township is one of 13 political units stretching from the Hudson River to the western Catskill Mountains, has long attracted summer visitors; now skiing is a winter attraction. The increased interest in the utilization of the Hudson River for recreational purposes attracts many motor and sailing enthusiasts to Coxsackie and its environs.

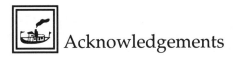 Acknowledgements

The loss of the Township official records in the 19th century major fire on Reed Street has been a handicap not easily overcome. Fortunately, the archival material in the Greene County Historical Society's Vedder Memorial Library in some measure substitutes as a primary resource. Beer's *History* of *Greene County* (1884), and Robert Henry Van Bergen's *Ye Olden Time* are useful secondary resources, although not always free of errors. *The Greene County News* column " Echoes of the Past" provides additional insights. *The Coxsackie Standard* issues in the June Rose Bedell Vincent Memorial Collection in the Vedder Memorial Library are equally helpful. The Greene County Historical Society (Bronck Museum and Vedder Memorial Library) is to be credited with sharing archival material.

Photographs depicting today's landscapes and their structures are provided through the expertise of Harvey Durham. Frances Dietz has been of major assistance, utilizing her skill at proofreading. Both individuals are vitally interested in local history and have been generous with their time.

Several townspeople have offered encouragement and assistance. Among these are Frances Adams, Ellen Whitbeck, Bill Bergman, William Tremmel, Joseph Garland and Henry Betke. Financial assistance in meeting a portion of the publishing costs comes from the Town of Coxsackie and is paid in lieu of the Town Historian's stipend. The National Bank of Coxsackie and the State Telephone Company, merit a special " Thank You" for similar assistance, they both having an important part in the historical development of Coxsackie Township.

Under Three Flags is dedicated to the late Daniel T. Monahan of South River Street, Coxsackie, who constantly urged the author to produce such a volume.

Raymond Beecher
Town Historian
Coxsackie, New York

The Coxsackie Quadrangle

Today's residents in the Township, except for experiencing the infrequent earth tremor or severe storms of wind, rain, sleet, hail or snow, have little comprehension of the gross forces which shaped their natural landscape over a period of some two billion years. Yet, to the keen observer, such evidences of geologic change are readily discernible, especially where man and nature have cut into the earth's surface. Power actions such as the continental drift and collision, the uplifting of land masses and their subsequent erosion, the various invasions and withdrawals of the salt sea, as well as the climatic changes caused by the mile-thick ice sheets which advanced and retreated at least four times, are all matters of pre-history. Finally, after eons of change, this Lake Albany region stabilized and provided a supportive habitat for migratory Paleo Indians.

A specific interpretation of the Coxsackie Quadrangle was provided by Dr. Winifred Goldring in 1943. She identified three distinct belts of land: (1) the Hudson Valley lowlands, some five to eight miles in width in Greene and Columbia Counties, much of which had been subject to intense pressures, and brought about a forty to seventy foot slant. Here are found extensive deposits of yellow and blue clay and sand beds; (2) the Kalkberg which rises to a height of between one hundred and three hundred feet, with a noticeable eastern escarpment. Here also the shale and limestone underwent intense pressure, being shaped in a north-south direction; and (3) a third belt, beyond the Climax limestone ridge, was composed of Hamilton sandstone and shales, all part of the eroded Catskill escarpment on the west.

The various small hills or drumlins, glacially formed, and the in-between low lying water-logged areas, are discernible today in belt three in the Climax-Earlton sections of the Township. Some hills such as Flint Mine escaped being covered by the late Ice Age, hills composed of shale, grist and chert. South of Coxsackie Village, on Route 385, are to be found Lampman and Klinkenberg Hills, prime examples of glacially formed natural landmarks.

The Amerindian Culture

A widespread stretch of eastern North American territory, including the Hudson Valley, Long Island, New England, Lower Canada and the Middle Atlantic area, was populated by prehistoric "red men" who called themselves the Lenni Lenape, thus identifying themselves as the original inhabitants. The most dominant were the Mahicans, who controlled a stretch of land some seventy-five miles east of Albany along the eastern river shore; their council fire was at Schodack. Prior to the white settlers' coming, these culturally related groups were all well-established by 1,000 A.D. We know them collectively as the Algonquins.

To the west of Albany and beyond the Catskill range lived the Mohawks. Armed conflict between the Mahicans and the Mohawks is a matter of pre-history. The legendary pitched battle between the two opposing forces on either Rogers Island or Wanton Island illustrates their bitter enmity.

The Katskill Indians, considered a subtribe of the Algonquin nation, occupied the lands comprising the eastern watershed of the Catskills, from Saugerties northerly and including most of the Coeymans Patent. Above the Katskills were the Mechkentowoons. The Katskill Indians tended to neutrality where possible. Henry Hudson described them as " the loving (peaceable) people." Governor Stuyvesant would use them to help mediate the bloody Esopus Indian War of 1655-1663.

Evidence of the several stages of Amerindian culture is plentiful in the Township of Coxsackie. As industrial and residential development continues, new sites are being uncovered. During the earlier years of this century, when Dr. Albert W. Parker both explored and summarized his Flint Mine Hill work, American archeology was still in its infancy and consequently many conclusions about Amerindian culture were oversimplified. Theories and methods of the "new archeology" which draw upon multidisciplines, are best typified by the remarkable excavations of the Koster settlement near Kampsville, Illinois. Since 1968, that activity has provided a vastly improved scientific understanding of America's prehistoric past.

There is a mild disagreement as to the inclusive periods of North American native pre-history, although most scholars accept the following time frames:

Pre-Paleo Indian - from about 30,000 to 12,000 B.C.
Paleo-Indian - 12,000 to 8,000 B.C.
Archaic Indian (Early, Middle and Late) - 8,000 to 500 B.C.
Woodland Indian - 500 B.C to recorded history

In actuality, these time classifications overlapped; they also have subdivisions. The Paleo-Indian groups were primarily big game hunters using spearlike weapons with projectile points; the distinctive "Clovis Point" was a product of this division. Except for stone artifacts, little survives from the Paleo-Indian culture since these groups were small migratory units. Paleo-Indian encampments existed in the vicinity of the headwaters of Coxsackie Creek and on the clay flats south of the Village.

The Archaic Indians managed a subsistence existence by hunting smaller game; by fishing the numerous streams, lakes and the major rivers and by gathering wild edible foods. During the transitional period leading into the Woodland classification, these groups utilized crude stone utensils but slowly practiced ceramic techniques. The Woodland stage brought the advanced development of the ceramic clay pot. The Archaic Indians populated the Coxsackie flats and the more fertile narrow valleys. They are known to have established semi-migratory sites on the East Ridge about one-half mile east of the Flint Mine Hill. One of the best examples of a Woodland village is that at Four Mile Point. These Indians had semi-permanent habitats and only shifted location as fertility declined in the tilled soil.

For thousands of years the Algonquin mines furnished immense quantities of quality flint-cores. Mine Berg (Flint Mine Hill) carries the prestigious Archeological District, National Register of Historic Places designation since November 29, 1978. Composed of grit and white weathering chert, its prehistoric importance is indicated by approximately two hundred flint pits, sorting and chipping stations, workshops and refuse dumps. (It is estimated that less than one percent of mined raw material was utilized in the finished stone product.)

That Coxsackie is an Indian name is beyond dispute; its orthography, however, is obscured by numerous Dutch-English translations. Neither was there any consistency of spelling until after the American Revolution. Generally, it is stated, these linguistically related eastern Indians used simple descriptive labels, frequently relating to some physical aspect of the area or a product found in abundance. Scholars of the old Algonquin language maintains that Earth was "ackey;" for the Mahicans it became "akek;" the related Delaware Indians used "haake," "aki," and "akhki." Thus translators concluded "acki" or "ackey" means "place of." Nutton Hook across the Hudson from Coxsackie was called by the Indians "Kochhackchungh," a nomenclature of some similarity.

The Bronck Indian deed of 1662 specifically mentions the land called by the Indians "Koxhackung;" the Coeymans Patent of 1673 indicates that location as "to the north of a place called by the Indians Koxhaexy." As early as 1872,

E.M. Ruttenberger in his scholarly book *History of the Indian Tribes of the Hudson River* posed the problem of Coxsackie's meaning. He quotes O'Callaghan who indicated the name to be a corruption of the Algonquin "Kaaks-aki" from "Kack," a goose, and "aki," locality - thus place or country of the wild goose. Schoolcraft defined its meaning "as place of cut banks" since here the river current is deflected against the western shoreline with erosive effect. The Algonquin dialect "A gooks Aki" was spelled "Kacks Hackie" by the Dutch. On an original map of 1800 the name "Kackhacken" or "Kachacle" appears, its puzzling literal translation means "cooked food in a bag." Another interpretation is "Cooksockuy" signifying owl-hoot. In the early 1700's Justus Flaukner used "Kockshagki," while in 1766 Peter Hoogteling in an affidavit stated that "Coxhackeye" is a flat, and it was in ancient times called by the Indians "Monaksackik." The Reverend Delber Clark in 1937 stated Coxsackie derived from the Indian "Mak-kacks-hack- ing" meaning place of many owls. Others believed "Co-aki" was a reference as heretofore mentioned to the clay banks fronting the river.

Yet an entirely different interpretation came from noted Indian archaeologist Dr. Albert W. Parker, who wrote extensively on the Flint Mines. He felt the frustration experienced by workers when a flint object was broken in the later stages of manufacture. This frustration is reputed to have inspired their strange amulets, the few found on site usually depicting a serpent devouring some animal. He concluded: "The name Coxsackie may thus have originated from the Indian words "Ahgooks" (or shooks) and "aki," meaning "Serpent Place."

French's *Gazetteer* (1860) reminded its readers that the Town's name was pronounced "Cook-sock-ey," being derived from an Indian word signifying "owl hoot." The "hoot of the owl" or "owls in the dense woods" has furnished Coxsackie with a current logo of interest. Since even the best scholars have not agreed to Coxsackie's exact meaning, and the Anglo-Dutch used over sixty spellings, Coxsackians today are privileged to accept the meaning they prefer.

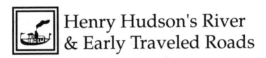 Henry Hudson's River & Early Traveled Roads

Weighing anchor and taking advantage of the incoming tide on the early evening of September 16, 1609, Captain Hudson and his Half Moon crew are presumed to have left the Athens area, sailing upriver. A narrowing channel with shoals, as well as oncoming darkness, dictated caution. The crew cast anchor and remained until daylight. On the seventeenth they sailed six leagues higher and eventually anchored all night. This is the closest we can come to the beginning of Coxsackie's recorded history.

No study of the Township of Coxsackie can ignore the influence of its location on the west bank of the Hudson, a river named by the English for its explorer. To Hudson himself, it was the "River of the Mountains;" the French consequently used "Rio de Montagne." The West India Company stockholders and highly placed Dutch officials thought it a matter of body politic to honor their stadholder, Prince Maurice of Nassau, by calling it Mauritius River. The settlers found it convenient to use the label North River to distinguish it from the East (Connecticut) and South (Delaware) Rivers.

To the Mahicans living along its banks, this "river of continually flowing waters" was the Mahicantuk, although the more warlike Iroquois to the west used the designation Cohatatea (Cohotate) meaning "the river which flows two ways."

Coxsackie in prehistoric eras was on the main north-south Indian route. This footpath came north from Cementon, crossing the Catskill Creek near Jefferson Heights. On the flats it paralleled the Limestone cliffs (the Kalkberg) until it reached the Hannacroix, where it passed out of the Township.

It is said that the Dutch farmers had little interest in public road building, being satisfied with crude wagon tracks to and from their isolated boweries. This appears to have been the rural policy throughout much of the seventeenth century.

By 1710, however, the English Crown, through the Governor's Council, determined that for both military and civilian needs, two main roads should be constructed lying on both sides of the Hudson River. It is the west one which is of special interest to Greene County and the Township of Coxsackie. As laid out, it came down from Albany, reaching the outskirts of West Coxsackie (then the only settlement here) by the bridge over the creek, on across the flats, skirting the eastern hills and eventually reaching Old Catskill (Leeds). From there it led to a ford of the Catskill Creek and on to the Kaatsbaan and eventually to Esopus (Kingston). When it finally left New York, it continued through the Jerseys. Until the Revolution it was the only major land thoroughfare connecting this vast expanse of west Hudson territory.

West Coxsackie and Old Catskill were the only semiurban settlements along the King's Highway in this section of what was Albany County, centers for trading and religious services. The King's Road has been compared with English and Irish thoroughfares of the eighteenth century - roads interspersed with farmsteads, taverns, blacksmith shops, houses of worship, grist and saw mills. Christopher Colles in *A Survey of the Roads in the United States of America*, 1789, is presumed to have utilized his earlier Revolutionary War survey of this King's Road he had made for the Continental Army. Identified in the Coxsackie map section are the Van Valkenburg and Konyn (Conine) taverns, the farmsteads of the Brunk (Bronck), Collier, Horbeck, Fosburg (Vosburg) families, the Kooksachke Meeting House, as well as Colonel Anthony Van Bergen's stone residence on the Coxsackie Creek.

The Reverend Delber Clark, a local historian, long had been puzzled at the lack of a major river connection with West Coxsackie during colonial times. He concluded that incoming and outgoing shipments of riverborne commerce were handled at Klinkenbergh (Four Mile Point) and hauled overland between that Landing and Coxsackie's only settlement. Such a crude road would have followed the 1864 route of the Saratoga and Hudson River Railroad. Eventually Van Dyck Street became a connecting link between West Coxsackie and the Upper Landing, Mansion Street on the flats then being blocked by swamp and bog.

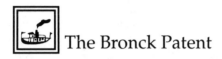 The Bronck Patent

Land was wealth to the early settlers of New Netherland-New York. Securing good title was the result of a combination of useful political connections as well as having the financial resources to pay off aboriginal claims. Having a history of military service against the French was a helpful factor. The Dutch West India Company issued many Grants of Land, sometimes without regard to Indian territorial claims. When the New Netherland colony was surrendered by Peter Stuyvesant to the English in August, 1664, by the third article of capitulation it was agreed "that all People shall continue free Denizens, and shall enjoy their Lands, Houses, and goods, wheresoever they are within this country and dispose of them as they please." The more cautious proprietors, however, petitioned for confirmatory patents, especially since the colony had been reconquered by the Dutch in 1673 and then once again restored to the English by the Treaty of Westminster signed the 9th of February 1674.

In the main, first as Duke of York and then after his succession to the throne, King James approved many grants, usually under delegated authority to his Governor of the Province of New York. This continued to be the Crown practice until the outbreak of the Revolutionary War. Attempts to restrict land grants to not more than one thousand acres for any one person generally were circumvented.

Fees charged for the securing of a land patent and annual charges of nominal quit-rents thereafter were sources of colonial revenue. In 1786 the New York State legislature authorized the extinguishing of such quit-rents by the payment of outstanding arrears and an additional fourteen shillings to every shilling of annual dues. Leonard Bronk was to handle this settlement for the Roseboom Patent heirs.

Pieter Bronck followed the land purchase procedure favored by Dutch Director-General Peter Stuyvesant. After first scouting available land not already patented, Bronck negotiated with the Katskill Indians and their legal representative, Johannes La Montagne, for a tract called by the Indians "Koixhackung." The contract "to buy and sell" was signed at Fort Orange (Albany) on January 13, 1662, by Indians Sisetas and Sachamoes as well as Pieter Bronck. The price was set at 150 guilders in beaver skins or the equivalent, with final payment to be made by May 1, 1663. Specific mention is made in the contract of the cleared land "being a way in the woods." Witnesses who also signed were Jan Verbeeck, Pastor Frans Barentse and Jan Dareth. Pastor Barentse was to hold a special power of attorney during Pieter Bronck's sojourn that late spring and summer at his Coxsackie bowery, where he was to clear more land and construct a habitation, one which turned out to be a North European type stone structure influenced by urban experience. The adjacent creek was long called Peter Bronck's Kill.

The Bronck-Indian contract was confirmed by English Governor Richard Nichols on June 11, 1667, the land once again being referred to as "Koixhackung." The Minutes of the Court of Albany, Rensselaerwyck and Schenectady, as translated by A.J.F. Van Laer, indicate that Dirk Hendrixse in 1666 was residing at Coxsackie "and that with Pieter Bronck and the Indian proprietor, who had sold the land of Coxhacky to the said Bronck, he went to mark the limits. First they came to a Steene kill (Stone kill), which come out of the great spring (groote fonteyn), and there marked a tree; thence, eastward, they marked (the bounds) to a point of a hill called Styfsink, and from Styfsink to the river, coming out a little below the Hoy Hoek, near a little kill on the west shore, opposite the lower point of the great Neuten Hoek, all of which was marked by the Indian, Shakamoes, and himself and Pieter Bronck, and he received the last payment when he had made the said marks. This purchase and marking took place before Jan Cloet and his companions bought their land (Loonenburg Patent) from the Indians, for Pieter Bronck was the first purchaser of this land in question."

Pieter Bronck and his wife, Hillitje, who settled on the cleared Indian acreage, are recognized as Coxsackie's first permanent white settlers, even though they wintered in Albany. While the passage of years has covered Pieter with an aura of historical glamour, he was actually a hot-tempered, contentious individual constantly involved in disputes. Born at Jonkoping, Sweden, in the Province of Smoland, in the year 1616/1617 (Julian Calendar date adjustment), Pieter from an early age supported himself as a sailor. It has now been established that Jonas Bronck, although not his father, was a close relative. We find Pieter Bronck at New Amsterdam at the time of Jonas Bronck's death in 1643. That same year Pieter made written reference in his own will that his parents "were far from here," implying they were still living in the Old World.

A few months subsequent to helping inventory Jonas Bronck's estate, Pieter sailed to the Netherlands. There he married Hillitje Jans of Quakebrugge, both being twenty-eight years of age. The couple was soon sailing back across the Atlantic. In 1649 these Broncks were residing in Albany, where Pieter built his tavern, the third in the settlement, and here son Jan was born about 1652. It is also said these "early Dutch" were a quarrelsome lot. If so, Pieter was a prime example. His tavern and brewing operations were subject to court criticism and his readiness to settle personal quarrels with "knife and fisticuffs" is a matter of record. Financially embarrassed in one of the early depressions, he was unable to pay his creditors. In that financial debacle he managed to save his Albany house but little else. He saw the establishment of a bowery at Coxsackie a means of providing a livelihood for wife and offspring.

While Pieter Bronck became Coxsackie's first white settler, Marte Gerritse Van Bergen (? - 1696), having superior financial resources and stronger political connections, had been actively acquiring patents of land in what was to become Greene County. He also added to these extensive holdings by purchasing the most northerly section of the Loonenburg Patent known as Fountain Flats. In doing so he came into conflict with the Broncks over the matter of boundary lines. After court hearings and personal negotiation, Jan Bronck and Marte Gerritse Van Bergen merged their territorial claims, the result being the issuance of the Coxsackie Patent of May 23, 1687. While much of the Fountain Flats land was subdivided and sold off at an early date, the Bronck and Van Bergen heirs continued to hold the acreage at the river in undivided common tenancy until the post-Revolutionary subdivision of 1784.

Four other land patents are of interest although some are only partially in the Township of Coxsackie: the Roseboom Patent of 1751 lies west of the Bronck Patent and northerly of the Catskill one; the Matthias Houghtaling Patent of 1697 extends from the Stoney Kill on the south to the Diep Kill along its northern boundary; the Stighkoke Patent of 1743 is a two-mile square grant in the Earlton area; the Coeymans Patent of 1673 (reaffirmed 1714) lies north of the Bronck or Coxsackie Patent, and until that boundary dispute was settled, overlapped the Houghtaling claim. Small plots of acreage also may be included here — Casparus Bronck's One Hundred Acres by mischance not included in other earlier patents, as well as a small portion of the first grant to John Morin Scott.

From the beginning, African-Americans were an integral part of the colony. The West India Company first set the example of importing slaves to work on the military fortifications, public buildings and company farms in New Netherland. Their justification for this was their inability to secure white laborers. Stuyvesant, among the largest of the slave holders in the colony, viewed this enforced labor as essential to the growth of New Netherland.

"Free negroes" might serve in the militia, own white indentured servants, and otherwise participate in the colony's affairs. Many slaves were granted "half freedoms" of full personal liberties as a reward for years of service. The African-Americans generally were regarded as a part of the human makeup of the colony; many qualified for church membership. Their close, familial relationship with the Dutch settlers continued down the decades, even under English rule.

African-Americans numbering more than four thousand served in the Revolutionary Army, with many more in local militias. Three years of such military service earned freedom by law. The New York State Legislature in 1781 passed the first manumission act pertaining to "earned freedom" for service in the late war.

It was Aaron Burr who led the legislative fight for immediate abolition of slavery in New York, but he lost out to those favoring a more gradual emancipation. Anti-slavery agitation continued to surface after 1785, aided by the New York Manumission Society. By law, passed in 1799, all males born of slave mothers after July 4, 1799, were to be free at the age of twenty-eight; females would gain their freedom at age twenty-five. As the years passed, the Legislature continued to eliminate slave restrictions until, in 1817, it enacted a law which provided for the final eradication of slavery in New York.

Coxsackie in the Revolution

The Massachusetts troubles which led to the outbreak of armed conflict spilled over rapidly into New York. At first, Colonists had little thought of complete independence; rather their motivation was a determination to manage colony affairs free from interference by the English Parliament, a body lacking as it did overseas representation. The gradual breakdown in "law and order" heretofore represented by the Royal Governor and his officials brought into being Committees of Correspondence on the state, county and local levels. In 1775 each distric assumed responsibilities for securing Association signatures supporting a coordinated effort to persuade King George III to convince Parliament it was infringing on traditional colonies' privileges and liberties. The Coxsackie Association, for several reasons, had difficulty getting some individuals to sign the protest, a few indicating on the paper they signed "By Order." Why the Coxsackie Association document never reached New York City with the others is uncertain. One suspects the slow process of getting signatures. This Revolutionary period archival item is one of the much misunderstood papers to survive. Its wording is almost identical to those of other districts in the state; it is not a unique Coxsackie Declaration of Independence. As Mabel Smith, Greene County Historian, so often has pointed out, it reaffirmed the ardent desires of the population for reconciliation with Great Britian when the political dispute was resolved.

With the total collapse of Royal government in the colonies and the escalation of the military conflict, three levels of colonial troops were established. The Continental Line, an intercolonial army under the Generalship of George Washington, bore the brunt of the fighting. Next there were the state levies, composed of men drafted from local militias who could not be required to serve tours of duty beyond New York's borders. By far the largest military forces in New York were the local militias. Required by law, these local military companies dated from the years of the seventeenth century and could be called out in times of emergency to fight against the French in Canada and their Indian allies. Colonel Anthony Van Bergen was designated commander of the combined Coxsackie and Great Imboght Eleventh Regiment of Militia at the outbreak of Revolutionary hostilities; he served as its major.

Early in the Revolution, a contingent of Coxsackie men, including Leonard Bronk, marched overland to Johnstown to apprehend its nest of

Loyalists. Others, as a unit, saw service when Burgoyne's invasion was stopped at the Battle of Saratoga. Captain Philip Conine, Jr. was in command of a detachment of militia stationed in the Catskill Valley near today's South Cairo to guard against Indian and Tory raids from the west. Some officers and men saw service in the Mohawk Valley; a few were enrolled in the Line and compiled a record of military service downstate, in Pennsylvania and elsewhere. Except for a few isolated raids, the greater Coxsackie Township was spared the destructiveness of military campaigns and battles. Surviving documents in the Bronck archives reveal that the Township was a major source of supplies to feed and clothe the military and those civilians left destitute as a result of local battles.

The So-Termed Yankee Invasion

Revolutionary soldiers from New England and from the lower reaches of the Hudson Valley had a first-hand opportunity to acquaint themselves with the thousands of acres of undeveloped land available in New York. Even before the official end of the Revolutionary War with the Treaty of Peace, signed at Paris in 1783, these land-starved families were on the move. For some, the greater Coxsackie Township of the late 1780's was their migration goal. Unlike the Van Rensselaer patroonship, the Bronks, Van Bergens, Houghtalings, Ver Plancks, Prevosts and others were willing to subdivide and sell outright on easy terms. Much of the land in the hill country with its narrow fertile valleys was for sale, the Dutch having preempted much of the flat lands in the Hudson Valley. Most settlers came to farm on an individual basis; a few joined the unsuccessful cooperative Forestville Commonwealth effort northwest of today's Earlton. Tradesmen, having special skills, set themselves up as blacksmiths, mill operators, ship-builders, tanners, etc. Others saw economic opportunity in trading.

As mentioned heretofore, the earliest settlers were presumed to have used the Klinkenbergh Landing at Four Mile Point for wharfage, hauling to and from West Coxsackie over the Flats, thus avoiding the steep hills around today's Reed Street. It was the enterprising Eliakim Reed, who had sojourned for a time in both Dutchess and Columbia Counties, who by the early 1790's moved to capitalize on the potential for a river port at the foot of today's Mansion Street. The main street still bears the Reed surname. Robert Henry Van Bergen in *Ye Olden Times* states that the Van Bergens received lot No. 48 in the Coxsackie subdivision of 1784 and that after Eliakim Reed purchased a part of that lot he "built a wharf and small store house at the northeast corner of a ledge of rocks." A surviving indenture between Peter Van Bergen of Albany and Eliakim Reed is dated July 13, 1792 and verifies this information. It transferred Peter Van Bergen's interest in Water Lot No. 48 to Eliakim Reed, containing 35 acres of land and also Lot 25 of 52 1/2 acres.

Over the next few decades rock, brickyard debris and other fill provided building sites along Reed Street as far out into the Hudson River as the rocky ledge. Prone to flooding and frequently requiring subfoundation piling support, the stores and warehouses became the center of business activity for the Township, gradually eclipsing West Coxsackie, the original settlement. Reeds Landing became one of the busiest along the entire Hudson.

With the 1784 subdivision of the remaining Bronck and Van Bergen lands in the Patent, Lots 46 and 47 totaling about 49 acres, came into the possession of the Bronck heirs. On March 7, 1794, Peter and Richard of that family surname sold these two large lots of land to Catskill Township merchant Israel Gibbs. This general area along the river had been carrying the label "Molly Wells Point," she being an early resident there with dubious land title. After Wilson and Gibbs established their trading station at the Lower Landing and built their wharf thereon, local residents referred to the Lower Landing as Gibbs Landing for a period of time. Access to this river frontage below the hill was then limited to today's lower Church Street, the mud flats blocking any entrance or exit via Reed Street. Dr. John Ely is known to have utilized a section of land at the Lower Landing for his early sloop building enterprise. Here also Joseph Chaplin had his potash works.

Unsuccessful in his trading activities at the Lower Landing, by 1804 Israel Gibbs faced bankruptcy. In an apparent attempt to thwart creditors, his land and improvements thereon were sold to Elam Gibbs and George Wilson. Creditors successfully appealed to the Court of Chancery which, in February of 1805, issued a writ against Gibbs's real and permanent property. Sheriff Peter C. Adams was ordered by the court to seize and sell Gibbs's "goods, Chattels, land and tenements." In advertising the public vendue (auction) Sheriff Adams stated, "I have seized and taken a lot of land lying and being in the town of Coxsackie, with the appurtenances thereon belonging, formerly known by the name of Molly Wells Point, now in possession of Elam Gibbs and George Wilson." A few months later the firm of Wilson and Gibbs dissolved and after June 15, 1805, George Wilson carried on trading activities alone.

Subsequent real estate transactions indicate George Wilson briefly held title to at least two-fifths of the acreage until he shared title with George Lusk. Excepted from those deeds of transfer were the potash works of Joseph Chaplin and a plot of ground fourteen feet square wherein "Mrs. Nancy Gibbs and Paulina Gibbs are buried."

The Lower Landing experienced a real estate boom after 1810, when surveyor and attorney Abraham Van Dyck set off numerous small house lots. A number of Federal-style houses date from this period of building.

The chartering of the north-south Albany and Greene Turnpike in 1806, and the opening of the east-west Coxsackie Turnpike that same year, provided greatly improved land transportation links. The flow of commerce, especially from the interior, consisted of hay, grain, livestock, potash, barrel staves, shingles, lumber, fruit, cider brandy, butter in tubs and firkins, etc., and the return flow of manufactured goods called for more and more stores and warehouses at Reeds Landing as well as at the Upper and Lower ones. At first by sailing sloop and later by steamboat, Coxsackie's pace of shipping activity increased substantially during the early decades of the nineteenth century. The ferry connection with Columbia County was soon relocated from the Upper to Reeds Landing. Here an improved horsepowered vessel was put into operation. A more direct connection between West Coxsackie and the Middle or Reeds

Landing came into being with the filling in of a roadbed over the bog with tree trunks and fill; finally Academy Street (now Mansion) became a thoroughfare.

There were those who thought they saw the potential for substantial profit by subdividing a large parcel of land at the Upper Landing for a planned real estate development. To this elaborate plan they gave the name "Carthage." Although some building occurred, it never succeeded in supplanting the Indian name "Coxsackie" nor in outdistancing Reeds Landing itself.

In 1812, in preparation for his soon to be published *Gazetteer of New York*, Horatio Gates Spafford requested John L. Bronk and his law associates to prepare a description of the Township of Coxsackie. After giving its location, boundaries and watercourses, they wrote:

These streams supply an abundance of mill seats on which are grain and saw mills, fulling mills and carding machines. There is a small pond (Bronck Lake) 2 miles S.W. of the Village (West Coxsackie), which covers about 25 acres. In the W(est) the surface is broken and hilly but in the E(ast) part is level, with much fine plain, and a soil of light sand or sandy loam, and some considerable tracts of clay. Coxsackie was originally settled by the Dutch, who constitute a pretty large portion of the present inhabitants. In 1810 the taxable property amounted to 538,775 dollars, when the population was 4,057, including 164 slaves, and there were 376 senatorial electors (men eligible to vote for the higher officials). The land is principally held in fee (in nonrestricted title). There are 3 Landings on the Hudson, 3/4 and 1 1/4 miles apart, at one of which there is the Post Office. At these Landings are some houses, several stores and 3 sloops, and W(est) of these is the Village of Coxsackie, extending W(est) about 1 mile on a handsome plain. This Village has been principally built since 1800 and now contains, 1812, including the Landings, about 100 dwellings, 15 stores, and a handsome Dutch Ref. Church..... Its trade is very considerable and increasing, and a turnpike extending to the W(est) is thought to have greatly increased it in amount. A large part of the present trade is in lumber, and traders assert it enjoys superior advantages for shipbuilding, from the excellence of its timber near the water.

It should be noted that the 1810 census information was used by John L. Bronk and others before New Baltimore and the northern section of Athens were set off from the Township of Coxsackie. Bronk dates the growth of the Village from about 1800 while others favor 1790. Among the early Coxsackie merchants and traders during this initial growth period were Archibald McVickar, Richard McCarty, Simeon Fitch and J. B. Cottle.

The War of 1812 saw the call of local militia troops. Dr. Henry Adams and Dr. John Ely were appointed medical officers. Captain John D. Spoor, the noted surveyor and mapmaker, served with his men on the northern frontier at Sacketts Harbor, where he succumbed to camp illness.

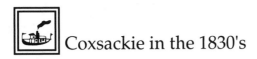 Coxsackie in the 1830's

By the third decade of the nineteenth century Coxsackie was a well-established community, so much so that Thomas Brigden Carroll, a son of a wheelwright Jonathan Carroll of West Coxsackie, was encouraged to begin printing a weekly newspaper *The Standard*. Upon the resignation of Ralph Barker, Coxsackie's first postmaster, this newspaper proprietor secured the postmastership appointment and removed the post office to his printing office. Carroll is also credited with establishing the first subscription or lending library in Coxsackie.

Gordon's *New York Gazetteer*, published in 1836, reveals a quarter century of growth since Spafford's 1812 publication. Gordon, like Spafford, referred to the Village as "being one mile west of the Landing," and then identified West Coxsackie as having "a Dutch Reformed Church, 7 stores, 2 hat manufactories, 3 powerful hay presses, 2 taverns, brickyards and more than 100 dwellings." Reeds Landing was now more extensively described as having "several wharves and docks, various streets upon the restricted margin of the river and the hill side, on which are 1 Baptist, and 1 Dutch Reformed Churches; 2 taverns, 22 brickyards; and an extensive hay press and about 30 dwellings; and 12 extensive stores and warehouses, several mechanics' shops, druggists, jewelers, etc.; and a printing office wherein issues of the *Greene County Advertiser* [are produced]. At the docks many sloops and canal boats are annually built and some steamboats have been constructed, and small ships occasionally hauled up for repairs. This is a place of much business employing 25 sloops, and having an export trade of more than half a million dollars annually in grain, cattle, sole leather, stone, brick, lime, clay, cord wood, etc."

Contact with the interior Township was being maintained by M. Hazard's stagecoach during the season of steamboat navigation. Local residents or those driving in from the rural areas of the townships by horse and carriage or wagon had a wide choice of mercantile establishments with which to trade. For those using the Upper Landing, Baker and Hall's general store and wharfage was the most convenient. Groceries and other supplies could be purchased at several village places including Olney F. Wright's, Smith and Van Schaack's, as well as Barker and Kirtland's (Henry Heermance in charge). Peter Hubbell and George N. Keith's store at Reeds Landing was a one-stop emporium, not only for provisions but also for dry goods, hardware and crockery. Some merchants such as Levi Hoag and Van Namee & Benedict dealt solely in dry goods.

Home sewing was the practice of many housewives who could examine bolts of cloth and purchase their needed yard goods and related notions at J. Wells located at the Lower Landing. Jas. C. Smith could also supply cloth and shawls. Newlyweds and others might select their furniture at Robert Carter's. Plain and decorated tinware was a specialty of J. Lusk while W.S. Jacks sold luxury goods including clocks and watches; he would also make precious metal dental bridge work. For saddles, harnesses and leather trunks there was a good selection at William K. Lusk's or at M. Vandenbergh's. Arthur Beatty was the place for boots and shoes.

Those needing medical attention could either request a house call or wait at Dr. W. D. Boardman's office adjoining Moses Powell's store or at Dr. J. C. Boardman's, he being the successor to Dr. John Ely's drugstore operation. Toothache sufferers could seek temporary relief by purchasing Kresote Drops at 50 cents the bottle. These were for sale at J. C. Dorman's at the Landing, at Stephen Truesdell's at the Village (West Coxsackie), or at Joseph Sherman's trading station at the hamlet of New Baltimore. Users were warned to keep the bottle in the box when not in use. Those needing legal services had a choice of Livingston and Spoor, R. W. Watson or Silvester and DeWitt.

The hauling of agricultural and forest products down to the Landings for transhipment required making arrangements with Captain Joseph Nelson's towboat Washington or Captain William Kirtland's Farmer, a vessel newly commissioned by Barker, Kirtland & Company. That same firm advertised passenger service on the renovated steam vessel New Castle.

Nicholas I. Lampman, who earned enduring fame for successfully completing the Bronck 13-sided barn, maintained an extensive machine shop in West Coxsackie. His augur patent for boring large holes in timbers for screws, presses and similar purposes, was being widely copied, much to his annoyance. John J. Powell was busy at his nearby two-story house and joiner's shop.

The stock financed Coxsackie Academy, newly completed, was advertising for scholars for its January 1837 term. The building was a convenient place for public meetings such as the one organized to encourage the Town to purchase and relocate the clock "now installed in the steeple of the Baptist Church" (present site of Christ Church, Episcopal.)

Epenetus Reed, one of Coxsackie's earlier successful entrepreneurs, was offering his sloop Congress, then berthed at New York, for sale on reasonable terms. Interested parties were instructed to contact him at his house on Ely Street where he lived in partial retirement.

Local businessmen were finding it increasingly irksome to have to do their banking at Albany, Hudson or Catskill; there was talk of establishing a bank. To that purpose a meeting was called for July 30, 1837, at the inn of William Mayo, "to take into consideration the establishment of a BANK at this place, under General Banking Law of this state." But local banking was delayed for another fourteen years, the Panic of 1837 being the culprit.

Sunday church attendance, membership in Bible societies, the support of domestic and foreign missions, and a growing interest in the temperance movement, all contributed to a somewhat moralistic climate of living during these early 19th century decades. Strangely enough, lotteries of all sorts were generally acceptable. The more affluent were attracted to the spending of their surplus money on literary publications or for a yearly five dollar ticket with the American Art Union. W. E. Leete was a lucky ticket holder in 1847, winning an oil painting by artist Asher B. Durand. The following year it was the turn of Miss Eleanor C. Heermance, who acquired Frederic E. Church's "Morning."

For generations the Dutch Reformed Church at West Coxsackie had served the community as a place of worship but with the growth of the Landings, other congregations became established. The Brick Church on Ely Street in 1833 transferred title to its building to the new Second Reformed congregation. The Methodist Church, organized in 1838, dedicated its building in 1840. The Episcopal Church, first established in 1806, never constructed a building. Finally, in 1853, during its reorganization, it first rented and then purchased the closed Baptist Church on Mansion Street. Saint Mary's Roman Catholic Church began holding services in a private home in 1845, their first church structure being built in 1847. Bethel African Methodist Church was organized in 1853 with the Reverend Lewis S. Lewis as pastor. Their church building was dedicated at the end of November, 1854 with an all-day service during which the Reverend Ellis preached in the morning and the Reverend Steele in the afternoon.

As commerce on the Hudson continued, vessels for freight and passenger service increased in size. Dusk and darkness no longer presented serious navigational hazards to "arrival and departure" schedules as long as the captains were certain of the location of the navigational channel. On May 23, 1828, the federal congress voted an appropriation of $8,000 for a light beacon and keeper's cottage to be located off the northern end of Wells (Rattlesnake) Island. The Four Mile Point funding would follow a year later, in 1829.

As constructed, the Coxsackie light made by seven lamps and reflectors arranged around two horizontal tables, cast a north-south beacon. This somewhat primitive lighting lasted until 1854 when the station was refitted with a sixth-order steamer lens and an argand lamp.

The Four Mile Point lighthouse was more controversial. The New York Collector of Customs at New York, Stephen Pleaston, in charge of these river beacons, approved plans for the acquisition of a tract of two acres on the west bank of the Hudson; it included a small stone house. Then the current landowner, William Jerome, wanted to sell only enough space for a light tower, hoping to collect a yearly rental for his stone house which could be occupied by the light tender. Threatened with a formal request to the State to commence eminent domain proceedings, William Jerome finally acquiesced to the sale. The Four Mile appropriation of $4,000, half of the Coxsackie's light sum, was justified because of the Four Mile Point location on solid ground. Ruel Clapp was the 1831 contractor for the tower and living quarters of this lower Coxsackie Township station while Cornell and Althouse contracted to install the light.

Water-borne commerce was not the only concern in the 1830's. The

Coxsackie and Schenectady Rail Road Company, with an incorporation life of fifty years, was chartered May 15, 1837. The plan was to lay tracks from the Hudson River on the west shore "between the shipyard of William Mayo and Cuyler's Point." If there was any hope of getting this line operational, the Panic of 1837 killed that anticipation.

When Davenport's *Gazetteer* came out in print in 1842, its description of Coxsackie varied little from Gordon's of 1836, with the exception of the addition of a few more dwelling houses. The population of the Township in 1842 was given as 3,539 persons, a figure probably taken from the federal census of 1840.

The Pre-Civil War Decade

While the earlier enthusiasms of the local citizenry for toll roads such as the 1806 one connecting Coxsackie with Greenville, Oak Hill and beyond was dampened by rising costs of maintenance and lack of traffic, a new generation became captivated with the 1840's concept of plank toll roads. The publications of the period stressed the advantages of "the smooth, all-weather driving surface." Would such a toll road, this time via Earlton, prove a profitable venture? Would Greenville investors purchase stock?

Acting under the state law of 1847 authorizing the incorporation of companies to construct plank toll roads, the Coxsackie and Oak Hill Plank Road came into being on July 27, 1852. The legislature at Albany specifically authorized this corporation to borrow up to a maximum of ten thousand dollars in addition to selling shares of stock. Among the stockholders anxious to promote the economic prosperity of their townships as well as make a reasonable return on their investments were William Mayo, Roswell Reed and Leonard Bronk (son of Judge Bronk) of Coxsackie. Support was also forthcoming from Greenville as Lewis Sherrill, Josiah Rundle, Frederick Coonley, Russell Wakeley, Gideon Botsford and David Powell signed the stock subscription book.

Construction commenced and proceeded at a rapid rate — through to Earlton, on to Greenville, Norton Hill, Oak Hill and then connecting with the Susquehanna Turnpike. The plank road owners, needing additional capital, persuaded Stephen Tryon of Earlton to lend $8,500 as part of the $10,000 authorized by the legislature. He soon found out it was a dubious investment and sought relief from the court, having been promised one payment of $4,000 after one year and the balance after two, and getting nothing. Tryon won a judgment of $9,583.58 damages and costs; he proceeded to secure an execution against the plank road company and its assets. Unfortunately, the sheriff could only seize and auction off property totaling $3,434.04 in bids, in addition to covering his own fees. With the death of Stephen Tryon, his executor, Levi Freleigh, brought action against the stockholders as individuals. Some settled and in turn brought suit against those who didn't. It was a legal mess.

By 1856 the western section of the Coxsackie and Oak Hill Plank Road was abandoned. A second section in the Greenville vicinity was given up by the early 1880's, with the remainder abandoned in the latter years of that decade.

Plank road enthusiasm did encourage an 1853 effort to connect the Middle Landing and the Lower Landing with a timbered surfaced roadway, but after the 1806 and 1852 efforts, Coxsackie would not become involved in any more turnpike concepts until the construction by New York State of the Governor Thomas E. Dewey Thruway. It then took years of effort to secure the Coxsackie- New Baltimore interchange.

The holding of Town Meetings, a political process which still operates in New England, was a state requirement for most New York townships in the pre-Civil War period, Coxsackie included. At least one Town Meeting was called for the first Tuesday in February wherein eligible residents voted by ballot for a supervisor, town clerk, justice of the peace, assessors, overseers of the poor, commissioner of highways, constables as well as two inspectors for each election, a third being appointed by the presiding officer at the annual meeting. Verbal yeas and noes sufficed for designating district road overseers.

Each Coxsackie road district was required to have its overseer of highways, heretofore called the pathmaster. Since there was no regular town highway crew, property owners were required by law to contribute assessed days of labor according to the size of their land holdings. Some participated with their hired men and teams while others paid the commutation money in lieu of labor; it was then the duty of the overseer to hire substitute manpower. He was also expected to warn his neighbors that the wayside weeds and brush had to be cut twice each year, once by July and once by September.

Although suggested for more than a decade, it was not until 1852 that a bank was established in the Township, its state charter dated March 14, 1853. The founding father was William Van Bergen Heermance who, for necessary capital, turned to his relatives in the Syracuse area — the Judson brothers. The latter family had been part of the Reeds Landing formative years until some removed westward to prosper in a variety of economic enterprises including banking. Hubbell Greene was appointed to the position of bank clerk in September, 1853. From the outset the bank prospered, although in 1862, during the Civil War, it was the target of counterfeiters who duplicated the one dollar note — a design of eagle and shield and a female feeding an eagle. At the close of the Civil War and with the establishment of a national banking system, this first Coxsackie bank became a part of that federal system.

Statistics from the New York State census of 1855 (except schools using 1858 figures) report that the Township of Coxsackie then had 17,698 1/4 acres of land under cultivation while 4,516 were considered unimproved. Real estate valuation was estimated at $782,710 while personal property holdings were certainly underreported at $165,334. Resident families totaled 491, of which 432 were freeholders in land title. The male population was counted at 1,891; it exceeded the female by one hundred. The thirteen school districts were providing educational facilities for 1,354 scholars who came from 592 dwelling houses.

Coxsackie's rural and more urban residents owned 635 horses of all breeds, while their working oxen and calves numbered 523. Many families had at least one cow for milk and butter, 791 cows being reported to the census takers. Of sheep there were 397 and swine numbered 1,565. Agricultural products raised on Coxsackie farms included 6,699 tons of hay and 44,796 bushels of grains. Potatoes were a staple, either for family consumption or for the market; Coxsackians grew over 17,000 bushels! The apple trees in the various orchards were producing 18,318 bushels of fruit. Cheese making had practically vanished as far as the market was concerned but butter was a major source of farm income; in 1855 over 83,700 pounds were produced. The milling of cloth had never been a Coxsackie Township specialty, although a few home looms were still in operation. The domestic cloth output was slightly over 500 yards, providing some business for the fulling mills then in a state of decline.

Coxsackie has had its share of natural calamities but few could equal the violent windstorm of March 18, 1854 which struck the Township. It was reported that "buildings were shaken to their foundations, chimneys shattered in reckless profusion, barns toppled and crashed in terrific confusion, trees were uprooted, fences blown down, and boards and shingles, borne by the blast, sailed through the air, endangering life and limb." For the Rufus Lasher family living on Mansion Street easterly of the Episcopal Church, it was an especially harrowing experience that night when the old Baptist Church roof began swaying, was uplifted, and finally broke up and crashed in pieces on surrounding residences, particularly the Lasher house itself.

 # The Civil War & Post-Civil War Years

By 1860 French's *Gazetteer* described Coxsackie as a place extensively engaged in brickmaking, and containing six churches, an Academy, a newspaper office, a bank, and several manufactories. It noted the decline in shipbuilding activity. For the first time, Jacksonville (Earlton) was listed as a hamlet in the western part of the Township.

With the outbreak of the Civil War, the 120th New York Regiment under the command of Colonel George W. Pratt assembled at Kingston and was soon ordered to the War Zone; a number of Coxsackie men were of that unit. In all, 82 soldiers have been identified as coming from the Township and serving in the conflict. The count of wounded, dead, and prisoners of war was a heavy one: Killed in Action - 4: Francis W. Dederick (Gettysburg), Captain Lansing Hollister (Gettysburg), George Sheffield (2nd Battle of Bull Run), Lewis Tucker (Gettysburg). Wounded in Action - 11: Theodore F. Bell (Chancellorsville), George F. Eldridge (Ceder Creek), Thomas Garrigan (Fredericksburg), John Hiseard (Spottsylvania), Henry Lamphere (Battle of the Wilderness), William Vandenbergh (Gettysburg), J. B. Van Wie (Gettysburg), Moses Walters (Gettysburg), and R. H. Whitbeck (Toloptomoy Creek). Prisoners of War - 7: Henry G. Bell (died at Andersonville), Martin A. Houghtaling (died at Belle Island) Died in Service not from enemy action - 1: Henry C. Collier

One of Coxsackie's heroes was John I. Spoor, a sergeant in the 120th. Early in action at Gettysburg, 204 of the 120th's 417 soldiers were killed. Captain Lansing Hollister and his two other officers were killed or put out of action, leaving Sgt. Spoor to lead the company, he being commissioned on the field to the Captaincy of Company D. The color bearers of the regiment were easy targets until Spoor's turn came. With the flag staff snapped in two from a shell, Spoor with his bare hands raised the 120th colors by joining the two splintered halves and carried the banner courageously.

Moving into the earlier post-Civil War decades, Coxsackie found itself part of a rapidly changing world. Many of those not in uniform had profited, either directly or indirectly, by the demand for both military and civilian goods. New agricultural output from the local small family-oriented farms and woodlots continued to decline as competition increased from the more westerly states. Larger steam-powered, metal-hulled vessels were beyond the capacity of the Coxsackie shipyard. Small grist and fulling mills were rapidly giving way to steam-powered plants capable of larger outputs. The scale of laborer's wages had risen as the war's inflationary aspects had cast their shadow on the economy.

The federal income tax, levied to finance the Civil War, continued after peace, although many were of the opinion it violated the federal constitution, especially the Bill of Rights. For the year 1867, sixty-one men living in the 10th Division, XIIIth District (Coxsackie, Greenville and New Baltimore) filed tax forms reporting income in excess of the one thousand dollar exemption. Many of these were from Coxsackie Township. Assistant Assessor S. S. Bell did not recognize the right of privacy when he released the sixty-one names and their taxable income.

Allen, Henry L. 500	Kidder, E. G. 959
Adams, F. G. 13,690	King, Thompson 12
Baker, William 200	Lampman, Obadiah 1,205
Bronk, Leonard 2,770	Lusk, Matthias 1,610
Brown, Isaac 1,006	Lusk, Gilbert 66
Brown, Hiram 500	Munn, Rev. A. F. 352
Bucklee, R. F. 500	McCabe, Edward 421
Bronk, E. P. 368	Mygatt, Calvin 72
Bentley, A. N. 316	Powell, Wheeler 2,172
Botsford, Gideon 94	Palmer, Epenetus 338
Conine, A .50	Reed, Alexander 1,642
Corey, Rev. G. H. 100	Reed, George 409
Cornell, T. F. 94	Reed, Wm. K. 366
Colbern, E. S. 660	Roe, Mark 593
Dwight, S. A. 621	Silvester, J. L. B. 982
Eaton, B. F. 233	Smith, John 4,412
Freligh, Levi 89	Salisbury, John 745
Fitch, Ezra1 23	Stoutenbergh, W. S. 36
Finch, B. N. 64	Spoor, M. (Estate) 1,778
Fuller, William 11,972	Stevens, Madison 582
Greene, F. S. 375	Story, Jacob E. 214
Hubbell, E. N. 224	Truesdell, John M. 405
Hollister, O. 189	Van Slyke, M. G. 225
Heermance, W.V.B. 1,066	Van Orden, W. T. 1,488
Hallenbeck, A. 68	Van Bergen, P. P. 143
Hamilton, D. M. 5,074	Vincent, E. H. 325
Hollister, Wm. H. 199	Vanderpoel, V. S. 564
Hotaling, George 220	Weeks, James 380
Hotaling, A. T. 168	Wing, Marcus 233
Hall, David 105	Wheeler, Wm. H. 101
Jones, Egbert 445	

The Coxsackie light station dating from 1829 to 1830, was on an exposed site, vulnerable to spring flooding and ice floes as well as continued erosion. By 1866, with the Civil War priorities eliminated, funding was finally available to rebuild the light's foundation, the base being supported by a substantial stone pier. The keeper's cottage was to be a two-story structure with the lantern tower in the northeast corner the tower rising 32 feet from its base. The lantern itself was to be equipped with a sixth order lens showing a fixed white light. The money was appropriated on July 28, 1866; construction was completed in 1868.

In May of 1867, the Village of Coxsackie incorporated, its population having grown to 1,341 persons, of which 734 were females and 607 males. The dwelling count was set at 197 houses which provided shelter for 305 families. West Coxsackie was determined to have its population of 300 persons included in the above; the same figure was set for the Upper Landing.

As real estate development increased, the distinct lines among the three landings and with West Coxsackie began to blur. Among the many building efforts were those of Henry McGuiggans who, in 1868, was erecting a double house in the south end. James Roberts, also speculating in a two-family structure on Lafayette Avenue, looked for potential in rental income. On a site overlooking a wide expanse of the Hudson River and surrounding countryside, retired dentist from the South, Dr. N. Clute was awaiting the completion of his elaborate Italianate residence off Ely Street; he would move into it in July, 1869.

Downtown's image was enhanced by the opening of the new quarters for the Coxsackie National Bank; that date was in the fall of 1868. The public was being informed the new vault was practically finished and the second floor was being equipped with office furniture and fixtures. By mid-December of 1868 the newspaper readers also learned that the Coxsackie Savings Institution was now open for business and was ready to accept all deposits over the counter of the National Bank. They were prepared to pay interest at the rate of five percent per annum.

Frederick T. Adams (1854-1910) at the family's Meadow Ridge Farm south of the Village convinced his young cousin, Roswell Reed Fitch, that they should recruit members for a boat rowing group. Thus the Alpha Boat Club of Coxsackie came into being. Other members were Myron Hubbell Greene, C. P. Wing, S. W. Briggs, P. Houghtaling and J. L. Myers. During July and August of 1869 these men could be found using their six-oared, 46-foot- long, 2-foot-wide, rowing scull Atalanta; Adams served as coxswain with Fitch as "stroke" and Myers as "bow captain." (Frederick Thompson Adams would, in later years, purchase the sailing sloop Sachem from Sir Thomas Lipton and with a volunteer crew unsuccessfully race for the international yachting trophy. He had a seat on the New York Stock Exchange and was also a popular commodore of the New York Yacht Club.)

Cochran's Grove, west of Washington Avenue, was a popular recreation place that 1869 summer as special events were scheduled, one for the local band seeking to raise funds for uniforms. Tickets were sold for both day and evening events. Food stands, a dance platform, a comedy-sketch by the "Hufta, Gufta, Lafta Society" plus an atmosphere made festive by the use of Chinese lanterns and torches helped to raise $255.

The Young Men's Association, Myron Hubbell Greene serving as president, sought to promote the cultural tone of the Village with a series of lectures to be offered during the winter months of 1867-68. Tickets for the ten events were offered for $2.50 "for any one gentleman with two ladies; single ladies' tickets could be procured for $1." Late comers or those objecting to the $2.50 seasonal cost, might take their chances at single-door admissions for 25 cents the lecture. The public-spirited younger men also maintained club rooms in a block on the east side of lower Mansion Street.

Local amateur baseball teams could get up a game at short notice. Coxsackie's Actives could always depend upon a contest with the Athenian White Elephants. If the game was scheduled for the east side of the Hudson, the Heermance Steam Ferry was prepared to provide crossing according to its published time schedule. Riders were warned, however, that "crossing the briny deep" now would cost 25 cents!

No greater medical controversy ever raged in the United States than the one between the traditional practitioners and the homeopathic school of medicine followers. Dr. C. N. Wetmore was now (1868) accepting patients who wanted the traditional medical treatment; his office was in the second house next to the Malleable Iron Works on Mansion Street. Dr. William D. Sprague, who stressed the homeopathic approach, also performed surgery, and could be consulted at his office opposite the Eagle Hotel. The medical partnership between Drs. Greene and Collier was being dissolved by mutual consent, Dr. Collier retiring from the firm. With the sale of his house in Windham, Dr. C. Barnett was preparing to join Dr. Greene at Coxsackie on January 1, 1868. Dr. P. O. Williams, having a well-established practice of the traditional variety, was eyeing semiretirement. His Bible Class at the Second Reformed Church was so well appreciated that the members presented him with a coin silver, gold-lined goblet. (It would surface again in northern New York in the 1980's, its history being traced by the Vedder Library staff.)

Legal services were advertised during this period by E. C. Raymond, whose family resided at Raymond Hall in West Coxsackie (later Park Hotel.) The need for a new cemetery had risen, the plots in the Mansion Street site being sold out. But public effort was slow; Riverside would come in the next decade.

The residents of the Township, especially in the Village, were long to remember the storm of 1869. On Saturday, October 2, it commenced to rain and continued doing so through Sunday and into Monday; the total rainfall measured 7 1/4 inches. The Hudson rose rapidly, the incoming tidal height being one foot higher than ever recorded heretofore. Water rushing down the hilly streets including New, washed out lawns and walkways. Among the victims were Mr. and Mrs. Klebe, who watched with amazement as part of their dooryard disappeared from their New Street residence. River Street became a canal. The docks were submerged to a depth of three feet, with Buckee and

Brown's lumberyard afloat and its coalyards flooded. F. and N. L. Bouton's 3,100 bushels of salt in their storage building was another victim. Reed and Powell's operation was inundated as was the Larabee Hotel. A. and B. Newbury, who had carefully planned against such an event when they constructed their machine shop on South River Street, was awash. The brickyards, even on the upper levels, suffered severe damage. Brown and Wing lost the major part of their stock of paints, oils and varnishes. Mail service was disrupted as damaged bridges on the Hudson River Railroad line were closed to rail traffic.

Some conservative residents felt there was no end to suggestions being proposed for public improvements, there being a growing interest in identifying streets with signs and for the laying down of flagstone walks! In spite of opposition, much of this would be accomplished by the fall of 1874. The Catskill newspaper would summarize all this activity by writing: "Coxsackie is doing herself proud in the way of improvements. New buildings are being erected all over the place and sidewalks are going down with a rapidity that almost takes your breadth away. The first thing we know she'll be a city."

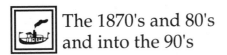

The 1870's and 80's and into the 90's

Coxsackie was still growing, the Catskill *Recorder* in February of 1870 noting that within the last eight months 27 new buildings were erected. On the mercantile scene changes were frequent. William Frear, now the Troy department store magnate, had downgraded his West Coxsackie establishment to branch status as Flagg and Frear; it had given him a millionaire's start. The Eagle Hotel, in 1870 owned by Captain John Smith, was sold on March 19 of that year to William Cummings. Mr. Bradbury, the hotel keeper, was leaving an establishment he had operated in top-notch fashion. Messers. J. M. Parker and Captain H. Salisbury were the new owners of the lumber and coal yard long operated by Isaac Mygatt. The Van Bergen interest in area grist mills, a family connection since the earliest pre-Revolutionary days, was declining. Robert Henry Van Bergen was advertising the Titus Flouring Mills for sale with forty acres of land, situated 2 1/2 miles west of the Landing.

The ice trade continued to prosper. By March of 1870 Coxsackie ice houses were just about filled to capacity. There were plans to stack out-of-doors should the cold weather continue. The merchants had benefitted that winter as workmen cashed in between $7,000 and $8,000 in ice wage tickets.

The Coxsackie, Greenville and Medusa Stage Line, now being operated by James Evans, was maintaining a daily run, except Sundays. Passengers bound for Greenville had a ride of 3 1/4 hours while those going to Medusa could anticipate a trip of 5 1/2.

Education in Coxsackie was again in crisis. Students were informed not to attend the Academy since Professor Cheeseman had resigned in order to take charge of a Collegiate Institute at Marion, Wayne County. The ladies and younger children might still attend Miss Olive Van Denburgh's Select School commencing February 1, she having set up in a house on Church Street opposite the Methodist congregation's Meeting House. The latter religious group was sponsoring a lecture by Mrs. Maggie Van Cott, of Catskill who was then in the process of establishing herself as one of America's noted female evangelists. Unable to be licensed in New York she announced she would soon depart for the West Coast to secure such recognition.

Plans continued for the establishment of a new cemetery. Alexander Reed, L. F. Botsford and William K. Reed were a committee of three authorized to secure and purchase suitable ground. The new cemetery was to come in 1873;

it would provide room for interment transfers such as in May of 1880 when Charles Sharp was informing the parties concerned that he had purchased the old Potash Burial Grounds in the Upper Village and was giving notice that buried relatives had to be removed to the lot provided in Riverside.

By a vote of 49 to 11, the Villagers on June 19, 1872, approved the building of a new firehouse. Baseball was still the main summer sport, frequently promoted by the volunteer firemen. A somewhat comic team named the Fat Men's Baseball Group had been formed.

Little could be done to put the Coxsackie Academy on a paying basis, the tuition being inadequate to meet operating expenses let alone paying the mortgage. The latter, originally held by Susan Bronk Van Bergen and renewed periodically, had finally been taken over by Leonard Bronk, then residing in Dr. Ely's house on Ely Street. On Saturday, October 21, 1884, the Academy land and building was sold at auction by Deputy Sheriff Chase; the successful bidder to protect his interest, was Leonard Bronk. It brought $6,000 over and above the face of the mortgage. Two years later, an Act of the New York State Legislature passed on March 20, 1886 authorized the Board of Education of the new Union Free School District No. 1 of Coxsackie to borrow money for the erection of a new school building and the payment for a site. The limit was set at slightly over $25,000.

Various sites were suggested for the new Coxsackie school but in the end the land bounded by Mansion and Elm Streets was chosen. Still situated on that site was Henry Greene's pillared Greek Revival residence. (It was E. D. Fancher who purchased a lot on Elm Street and arranged for the moving of this Greene structure to that new location. Many older residents remember it as the Kaksakee Inn, a place for banquets, dining and the renting of rooms.) The second Coxsackie Academy or Union School was opened to scholars in 1887; it would serve the community, with the addition of a two-room wing, until the opening of the present Coxsackie-Athens Central School.

Coxsackie Township had established health regulations to prevent the spread of diseases ever since the cholera epidemic of 1832, in which brickyard proprietor French was the first victim. Again, in 1854, a second cholera scare surfaced. Many health regulations came about as a result of state mandates.

At its regular meeting of the Town Board of Health held June 1, 1888, the various rules and regulations pertaining to public health matters were updated and ordered published. Present at that meeting were supervisor Alexander Cumming; Robert H. Van Bergen, Aaron Whitbeck, Isaac C. Hallenbeck and Edwin C. Hallenbeck, all justices of the peace; town clerk Edward C. Garrigan; and William E. Bailey. The *Regulations & Orders of the Board of Health, Town of Coxsackie* concerned themselves with such matters as the location and maintenance of privy vaults, disposition of offal or dead animals, fitness of food for human consumption, quarantines against infectious diseases, public funerals for victims of smallpox, diphtheria, scarlet fever, or typhus; and the registration of births, marriages and deaths. Fines ranging from five to twenty-five dollars could be assessed against violators of the promulgated regulations. The Public Health Officer, generally a medical man, was responsible for enforcing the health code.

In the summer of 1887, a young farm boy who had recently earned his high school diploma at Lisle Academy appeared on Coxsackie's Reed Street. His goal in coming to the Village was to learn the newspaper and printing trade under his cousin, William P. Franklin, who was then publishing the *Coxsackie News*. Little did the older cousin realize just what a dynamo he had enticed to the Village. "Whoop for Coxsackie" was to become young Franklin's slogan and "whoop" he did. In addition to working for his cousin on the newspaper, Herb Franklin soon had other irons in the fire. He recognized the growing interest in the adult use of the safety bicycle and established his own agency selling the Columbia. Next he was actively engaged in the buying and selling of real estate and insurance. In this latter project he was assisted by Frank F. Bedell.

The Board of Trade was another Franklin concept. Organized in 1889, he served as its secretary. He promoted the idea of buying the old foundry site on Mansion Street and enticed Kennedy Valve to relocate. Recognizing the adequate supply of female labor, he was behind the Board of Trade's promotion for a shirt factory. Water and electricity were also municipal concerns of young Franklin.

It was the Underwood and Franklin team who developed a new process for casting metal under pressure rather than using the older open mould sand casting process, Underwood having come to Coxsackie with Kennedy Valve. This last business venture took Franklin and Underwood on to Syracuse where, under the name of the H. H. Franklin Manufacturing Company, the Franklin Finished Die Castings became a winner. His departure from Coxsackie was a loss not easily overcome.

The Board of Trade, as established in May of 1889, continued to promote the welfare of the Village down the decade. Was a paid police force a necessity? As with other proposals to increase the operating budget there were pros and cons for this additional expense. Building activity continued with the real estate firm of Franklin and Bedell offering three sites for sale on Washington Avenue, one already having a framed residence. On Mansion Street another owner was offering a "good building site" on which a barn already existed. Christ Episcopal Church vestrymen met at Attorney N. A. Calkin's office on July 16, 1892, to discuss the letting of a contract to build a rectory and a parish hall. It was hoped the work could be completed in time for Bishop Doane's next visit.

The flooding and ice floe damage which occurred in February, 1896, was another downtown calamity of nature. The ice dam forming at Four Mile Point, plus the rapid-run off of water, flooded the Landings. Rowboats were a necessity on Reed and River Streets. Even the National Bank staff, assisting the public, stood at their counters in several inches of water.

The End of the Century

The nineteenth century was winding down. To most it would end on December 31, 1899, not 1900. Coxsackie with its three river landings and railroad connections was still the hub for Greene County's northern section as well as for adjacent communities in the County of Albany. Stagecoach lines still connected Medusa, Norton Hill, Greenville, with the hamlets of Grapeville, Medway, Urlton, Climax and finally Coxsackie itself. J. W. Alverson and his drivers had the Medusa-Coxsackie route via Grapeville while S. Tousan & Company were operating over the Urlton roadway. That line commenced at South Westerlo and after leaving Greenville made stops at Greenville Center, Surprise, Result, and Climax before descending the hill onto the Coxsackie flats. A supplementary source of income for the coach companies was the transportation of United States mail, which came into Coxsackie from the south five times the day and from the north six times daily. In better weather the passenger traffic flow frequently required extra stage runs but if it was only an occasional extra passenger, that fare could occupy the driver's seat, the latter perching on the dashboard. These stage drivers were adept at cultivating the public's good will, especially of the female passengers. When Andrew Ellsworth, a popular driver, and his bride, came in as passengers on Joe Alverson's stage run, the trip was accompanied by the ringing of large cow bells attached to the coach while the public cheered them through from stop to stop.

The various companies providing river transportation for freight and passengers were reviewing their 1899 schedules in an attempt to snare as large a share of the market as possible. The Coxsackie, Albany and Newburgh Line planned to operate two vessels — the M. Martin (Captain Peter Acker) and the Jacob H. Tremper (Captain Jack Roosa). These two vessels were to run alternately with the Tremper responsible for the 4 p.m. Coxsackie upriver connection on Monday, Wednesday and Friday and the downriver one from its 10 a.m. stop at Coxsackie on Tuesday, Thursday and Saturday. "Particular attention given to delivery of orders, purchasing of goods, or business commissions of any description by either captain."

The shorter route between Albany and Hudson would include a quick call at Coxsackie by the Hudson, captained by Percy Wolfe with Henry Taylor and Vincent Marsh working the deck.

Other vessels also had their eye on the Coxsackie landing. The little steamer Charles A. Schultz commenced in a big way the spring of 1899 to transport passengers on the run between Coxsackie and Athens, and Athens and Hudson. Four trips the day were at first scheduled but this was later reduced to three. By midsummer the Schultz was pulled off the route, blame being placed on "insufficient traffic."

The Coxsackie, Catskill and New York Line was a major competitor on the river. It would run the Kaaterskill and the City of Hudson from Reeds Landing, the McManus from Stuyvesant and the Onteora from Catskill, the latter under command of Joel A. Cooper of Athens.

During the winter of 1898-1899, the ferry scow pulled by horses provided passenger connections with the east shore railroad. Some brave souls chose to walk over the ice but this could be a chilling effort. By early spring, as the ferry sleigh kept breaking through the ice every few rods, Captain Charley Van Slyke deemed it time to start up the steam ferry.

The Hudson River's 4-million ton ice crop harvested over the winter of 1898-1899 was the largest ever and provided many local ice field hands with cash income during the lean agricultural months. Their spending provided retail merchants with extraordinary sales. The independent local ice house operators were becoming increasingly concerned at the heavy competition from the Consolidated Company, which was dictating ice prices in New York. There was talk of holding Coxsackie ice crops over the summer season, the price being offered in 1899 being too low. Whether bluffing or not, some owners were keeping their houses heavily covered and were taking other precautions to insulate through the hot months.

On the local scene, a boon to busy housewives and single gentlemen was the downtown laundry service of J. E. Browne, Jr. Acting as agent for the Union Laundry and also McFarland's Dye and Cleaning Works, Brown stressed prompt service, the items leaving Coxsackie each Wednesday at 7 p.m. and available to the owners on Saturday at noon. John Frank's Furniture Emporium believed in advertising. His Spring special was a 7-piece oak bedroom set for $15. Shufelt and Titus were utilizing steam from the electric light plant to process their monument and other orders at the North River Steam Granite and Marble Works.

Six retail merchants had finally joined together to ban premium stamps as of July 1, assuring the housewife that their prices in turn would be lowered. To Winans & Bailey, C. I. Collier & Co., Richtmyer & Sax, S. H. Van Dyck, Clark & Hotaling and Michel Dolan the premium stamps were a nuisance.

Both merchants and housewives suffered from the dusty roads the summer of 1899, it being the driest in several years. Clouds of dust filtered through closed doors and windows, leaving thick coatings which required daily cleaning. The general lament was "Oh for Elias Palmer and his old sprinkling cart." Finally the situation became so intolerable that Ed. Cumming, Jr. filled up the old sprinkler wagon and solicited businessmen and private householders for donations to finance the daily sprinkling of the dust. "Oh for tarred roads" wrote the *Union* newspaper editor. "But progress costs money" was the reply, and taxpayers were reminded the Village yearly budget had already reached the high figure of $6,700.

With increased freight and passenger traffic, the West Shore Railroad was becoming a key transportation route. Danger to crossing pedestrians, their horses and vehicles was ever present. From 7 a.m. to 7 p.m. the traveler could depend upon the crossing guard working the gates but nighttime was a different story. To protect both the public and itself, the Railroad erected a large sign at the Mansion Street crossing warning the public that they crossed at their own risk during the 12-hour period from 7 p.m. to 7 a.m.

At this busy section of Coxsackie, pedestrians frequently had to utilize muddy paths, there being no flagstones. To accommodate the public and perhaps increase custom, a plank walk was laid down from the Coxsackie Hotel fence corner to the front door of the West Shore Hotel. The latter establishment was not the only one in the Village to seek, by indirect means, to attract customers and establish good will. "Uly" Van Loan invested in one of the best gramophones and advertised free record concerts each Saturday evening at his Klondyke Hotel, South River Street.

The river signal beacon at Four Mile Point had a new light tender, Joseph Burke having been transferred from the Execution Rocks station in Long Island Sound. The government steamer Rose brought his personal property upriver in August. In the midst of a busy summer season the ferryboat's condition required its being pulled from the daily runs for emergency repairs at the Baldwin Shipyard at New Baltimore. Fortunately, that yard was able to make emergency repairs which restored service in a minimum of days.

The several churches held their summertime bazaars and ice cream socials as well as scheduled picnics for the Sunday Schools. The Second Reformed Church sponsored a boat ride to Baerena Island Park at Coeymans, children and parents being warned the tug Skinner pulling barge Merchant would cast off from Parker's Dock promptly at 8 a.m. Music would be furnished by the Crescent Band. The day's excursion was priced at 25 cents the passenger. Simpson's Grove in the Four Mile Point area was another popular summertime spot. St. Mary's congregation had more than socials on its mind as it contemplated building a more adequate house of worship. And the new pastor of Bethel A.M.E. Church, the Reverend A. W. Pierce, was now installed, having removed from Roslyn, Long Island.

Construction of commercial and private structures kept the town's carpenters and builders busy as the 1899 spring season progressed. Elias Gates broke ground for a new dwelling north of his present home at the Upper Landing. Sensing a growing Coxsackie need for housing, John Frank converted the old Reed orchard into building lots and also graded an entrance from New Street. Fred Goulde's skill at the trade was well known and his services in demand. In late May he had raised a 40 x 50 foot barn on what was known as the "Billy" Spoor place, now owned by Albert T. Hotaling. With the help of Abe Kent, finishing touches were put on the Thomas Bell tenant house near Four Mile Point while Charles Duntz filled his contract to do the plastering. Waiting to move in was G. W. Overbaugh, foreman for Bell Moulding. Thomas Bell of Catskill was busy reminding the local men that he had invested heavily in the Bell Ice House at the same location south of the Village and it was the first ever built by Mr. Anthony; it was pronounced by icemen to be one of the best such buildings along the river.

Some local businessmen renovated existing structures. William Shufelt improved his blacksmith and wheelwright shop on lower Mansion Street by raising the structure four feet and thereby creating a large second story room overlooking the river. The W. A. Edwards hardware store was changed over as a drug store to accommodate Jordan Brothers; the building would house flats on the upper story. The empty Backus store opposite the Eagle Hotel (at the foot of Mansion Street) was to be occupied by Jacob Zimmerman, who intended to make and sell his own line of candies. And some residents updated their private homes, among them D. Geroe Greene had a piazza added to his Queen Anne Revival style residence halfway up Mansion Street. (He also gambled on electricity being the utility of the future by having the entire home wired.) Added protection for the expansion of the Village and its surrounding rural area came with the filing of Articles of Incorporation for Hose Company #3, West Coxsackie, the sponsors being Samuel T. Burroughs, Benjamin W. Harden, Charles M. Palmer, Albert E. Finch and Arthur P. Whitbeck.

The James Sutherland store with its line of "Fruits, Vegetables and Confectionery" items had been sold to Cornell Vosburgh that year, who was busy selling out a portion of the inventory coming with the store's purchase. Vosburgh had a fine reputation for growing fresh produce for the market and was apparently attempting to secure a local retail outlet to maximize profits. With a good sense of humor, he began advertising a clearance sale, utilizing the forthcoming trolley line rumors. It did attract the attention of the local newspaper readers. Sugar could be had at 5 cents the pound, cans of Columbia River salmon at 15 cents, New Orleans molasses at 35 cents the gallon, Arbuckle Coffee brand at 13 cents the pound, while anyone with a spare nickel could scoop up a pound of oyster crackers or, for a dime get a package of pancake flour. (Millie Carrington recalls the Vosburghs in later years always would chuckle about the man who came into the store almost daily for a single stick of chewing gum.) Cheap prices or not, Cornell Vosburgh's mercantile endeavor in the Village did not last. After that he gave his complete attention to his fruit, vegetable and flower operation on Route 385, which eventually developed into Vosburgh's Nurseries.

C. W. Duntz, successor to H. B. Lampman, was the first Coxsackie coal dealer to handle soft coal for industrial purposes at his dock that summer. Also of interest was the March 1899 sell out by A. C. Sloan of a market wagon, cutter, sulky, harness, robes, pole-tongue, etc. Could he have foreseen the advent of the gasoline-powered vehicle promoted by his grandson, Alfred P. Sloan, Jr. of General Motors?

Mike Dolan was trying to compete with other merchants, his Opera House block being off the more visible Reed Street. To that purpose he contracted for the painting of his various store fronts including the Dolan shoe store.

The public was informed that James H. Lampman, for some months at New York preparing for duties as an undertaker, was now licensed as an embalmer and ready for business. He wanted the public to know he still was prepared to utilize the cold (ice) process for those not ready to accept embalming.

The turnover of business firms at Coxsackie was high, there being a variety of reasons, one of which was the lack of profit. August Schmidt's Columbia Hotel opposite the Coxsackie Fair Grounds closed its doors and held an auction of the contents in November. At the mortgage sale, J. H. Whitbeck made a bid for the real estate of $1,115.

Agriculture was still a main means of support for many families. Whenever possible the men and older boys augmented the family's cash position by seeking out jobs including work on the ice fields, lumbering or fishing. The farms tended to specialize in hay crops, fruit, milk and butter, eggs or vegetables. The Ely and Bronck Farms, owned by Mrs. Lewis Lampman, were pace-setters for local agricultural interests. Their Jersey herd of cattle was outstanding, and whenever surplus stock was sold off it attracted wide interest. One such sale came on May 13, 1899, when Jersey cows, yearlings, calves and bulls were auctioned off. Wagons, sleighs, harness and other equipment also fell under the hammer, all on six months' credit terms. Carlos Tompkins and family had moved onto the Bronck Farm to handle the butter making under the supervision of Will Currie. Having the financial resources to hold over the hay crop for higher spring prices and shortages at New York, the Bronck Farm manager was busy directing Fred Aley to move out three carloads of hay come May.

Dairymen throughout the Township and its environs were thankful that the Coxsackie Creamery, sold at mortgage foreclosure, had been purchased by John Brown of West Coxsackie and W. H. Miller of Athens. It was reopened with Levi Garrett, formerly of Stanton Hill, placed in charge of the butter making. But this good news turned sour when by mid-August of 1899 it was clear to the owners that the needed volume of milk from 300 cows was not forthcoming as had been anticipated.

Cold storage facilities for fruit was a means to securing higher prices. The Winans and Bailey cold storage plant was being partially emptied in early March, with a carload of apples being shipped to the metropolitan area.

 Into the New Century

The style of living was changing. Indoor plumbing, electricity and the telephone, once considered luxuries, were becoming necessities. The small family farm continued its economic struggle, with the main wage earner ever alert to the chance to earn a few cash dollars. It was a time when limited incomes could be stretched to meet normal expenses, particularly if a vegetable garden and canning were part of the effort. Many school taxes were under ten dollars the year for the districts' one-room educational programs. Rural Free Delivery, a new postal service, was a boon to rural residents, eliminating the need to call at the post office for mail. One of the earliest of such carriers was Edward Roberts who, in October of 1903, commenced distributing mail free to country people. His route included Roberts Hill, the Flatbush, Stanton Hill, the south half of the Coxsackie-New Baltimore Road — all told a distance of 21 miles.

For residents and visitors still dependent upon the horse and carriage or wagon, the railroads and steamboats were the answer to their need for rapid passenger and freight transportation to more distant points. Two daily steamboat lines, during the season, connected Coxsackie with New York and Albany, while another plied the shorter distance between Coxsackie Landing and the City of Hudson. The ferry connection, advertised as the shortest crossing between New York and Albany, was an added convenience for those meeting the New York Central trains at Stockport Station. The West Shore Line, with both passenger and freight stations in operation since 1883, was another option. Few residents could foresee the drastic changes in mobility forthcoming with the popularization of the automobile.

Family farms, many of them specializing in hay production, fruit, and dairying and poultry were slowly being overtaken by the taking in of summer boarders. In the Village itself, the ice houses, foundries as well as retail trade and professional services contributed to the residents' economic well-being. An analysis of the Village Directory of 1901 indicates it was still the norm for the male to earn the family's income while the wife performed the traditional homemaking activities. For those females needing to work outside the home, opportunities existed in teaching, clerical, light factory work, and in domestic cleaning. Dressmaking at home was another avenue of income, 16 women catering to that market.

It was a time of limited higher education, many completing their formal schooling at the completion of the eighth grade or at age 16. High school graduation classes in Coxsackie seldom exceeded ten scholars, most of whom were college bound. "Laborer" was the most common occupational listing in the 1901 Directory, 113 men giving that means of earning a livelihood. Step ups on the occupational level were the various jobs at the metal foundries: 36 foundrymen, 24 valve workers, 24 moulders, 15 machinists, 6 brass finishers, 6 coremakers, 3 polishers, and two pattern makers. A few more males were connected with these local foundries as timekeepers, watchmen, firemen, engineers as well as managers or proprietors.

The care and use of the horse meant work for blacksmiths, 17 being listed, possibly some retired. There were 18 cart and bus drivers, 2 harness makers, 1 coachman, 3 livery stable hands and proprietors, 11 teamsters, 4 truckmen, a wagon maker and a stage driver.

In the hamlets of Climax and Earlton (Urlton), the general store sufficed for daily needs but residents generally made one weekly trip into Coxsackie itself. Here the stores tended to specialize, there being newsrooms, candy and ice cream parlors, bakeries, meat and fish butcher shops, dry goods marts, mens and boys clothing stores and shoe retail establishments. Medical, dental and legal services were available in the Village. Doctors covered a wide area making house calls at all hours. In contrast with today, in the 1901 Directory only six persons were employed in the teaching profession. Each religious denomination had its own cleric.

In addition to several hotels, which varied in quality of accommodations, some housewives took in roomers and or boarders, especially during the ice fields' winter season. The Village was also a place of residence for retired couples and widows, some of whom moved in from the more rural areas. The 1901 Directory lists 81 widows "Not gainfully employed."

Friday evening into the late hours of Saturday evening were the big shopping periods of the week. Mark Richtmyer's recollections included Reed Street stores remaining open evenings until nine p.m., and on Saturday nights "as long as customers came in, at times close to midnight." The more progressive storekeepers such as Dayton Smith with his newsroom were lighted with acetylene fixtures. Awnings of wood and canvas both sheltered patrons from sun and rain, as well as protecting the merchandise on display in the store windows. On the north side of Reed Street, some shoppers coming in with wagons or carriages used the overhang support posts for hitching purposes. The wood and brick stores were generally well maintained, the Dolan interests being a leader in this respect.

The Opera House at the Landing offered paid entertainment but had some competition from the Day and Night Boats arrivals and departures, a sight of interest to many and all free. The Sabbath Day meant a cessation of commercial activity.

Reed Street stores frequently housed the owners' families on the second level with apartment rentals generally also available on top floors. Some buildings had office space on the above ground floor levels, requiring a climb up steep sets of stairs. This was especially true of professional offices, lodge rooms and the printing establishments.

As a busy river landing, railroad station, and stage terminal, Coxsackie had a continual demand for transient accommodations. Additionally, some men from the interior working the ice fields sought inexpensive overnight lodgings in the cheaper hotels. The Coxsackie hotels varied in size, quality of service and price. The Cummings men in their three-story brick hotel at the corner of Reed and South River had an interrelated operation, with Alex Cummings and his clerk, George Herrick, providing "special accommodations for traveling men who desire the best, including steam heat and electric lights." This establishment advertised itself as "one of the best two-dollar hotels along the Hudson." Ed. R. Cummings had his livery stable in the rear of the hotel yard while Daniel Cummings was in charge of the local stage line route between the Landings and West Coxsackie. He also served as agent for the National Express Company.

At the foot of Mansion Street, a hotel site for most of the 19th century, the New Eagle Hotel competed with Cummings' establishment. The Landings Klondyke Hotel, Uly Van Loan as proprietor, guaranteed first-class accommodations at one dollar the day; it was a popular place for ice crews. The Hotel Royal, 21 Reed Street, operated by G. H. Case and George W. Edwards, could apparently house a few transients on the upper floor but it was primarily the place to purchase wines, liquors, draught beer and cigars. The same might be said of Mike Dolan's Central Hotel.

The Larabee House, 1-3-5 River Street, was then under the management of Captain J. V. W. O'Connor. It made a point of advertising being "Near to the Ferry" and that telephone reservations could easily be made by asking the switchboard operator to ring number 17-2.

On Mansion Street in West Coxsackie, M. Prendergast, Jr. was proprietor of the West End Hotel, "in operation since 1870." He would also boast of electric lighting with room bell call service, "first-class pool tables and a bar supplied with the best wet-goods. The meals are substantial — Not All Style." His hotel was also a stop for all interior stage lines.

Trading horses was as important to most families as today's deliberations on the purchase or trade-in of the automobile. The more affluent families had their own carriage houses at the rear of their properties. The rural residents, of course, had their barns to house horses, carriages, wagons and sleighs. The Silvesters at West Coxsackie had their own coachman who cared for the animals and also had the responsibility of transporting the ladies. In the main, however, it was the husband and father who handled the reins or rode saddle, although a few more active females were equally competent with the horse and carriage. Accidents were frequently reported in the newspapers, generally not caused by a broken shaft or wheel but rather by scared runaway horses.

Residents unwilling or unable to care for their horses at home could arrange for hired "taxi" service with the various livery stables; Frank S. Vermilyea's was one. He had taken over the stables opposite the New Eagle

Hotel (foot of Mansion Street) at the death of William Kempton Reed in 1899. Here, "at reasonable prices," he was prepared to provide "first-class carriages with competent drivers for weddings and funerals or for sight-seeing about the county." Ed. R. Cummings, at his livery stable on South River Street behind the family hotel, also advertised that he kept "first-class rigs in readiment at all hours." He also was prepared to provide overnight stable housing for transients' horses and year round service for local residents not desiring to care for their animals at home.

Foremost as a commission dealer for livestock, especially horses, as well as for equipment of that sort, was William Woolford. His new sales pavilion was within a block of the West Shore depot. The importation of carloads of horses from the midwest was a frequent practice. One could always "shop around" for harness, saddles, as well as carriages, wagons and sleighs, either at Theodore J. Every's at the Landing or at J. H. Whitbeck's at West Coxsackie.

Powell's Express and Baggage Line was prepared to provide carting and trucking services giving special attention to the moving of pianos and furniture. Having no telephone at his home on Lawrence Avenue, potential customers were asked to leave messages at McClure's Drug Store, at the *Coxsackie News* office, at S. C. Bennett's or at the West Shore depot.

Coxsackie families, as well as those driving in from the country, had a wide choice of merchants with whom to deal, both at the West End and the Landing. Several merchants stressed free delivery service. John Lugert, at his Mansion Street West End bakery, catered to both the wholesale and the retail trade, selling bread, cakes, rolls, buns and pies. His delivery wagon clerk, Charles Sharp, had a daily sales route through the Village. Near Lugert's was F. H. Roberts selling choice groceries including tea, coffee, sugar, salt, fish, pork, lard, as well as flour in the various grades. He encouraged customers to trade, bringing in their eggs and butter for which he was prepared to pay the best market prices. In connection with his store he also maintained a free home delivery route.

In the Dolan Opera House block, with similar free delivery service, Ferdinand Ritz dealt in "choice family groceries, including food in cans." A sideline was wood and willow ware. (This long-lasting mercantile operation finally relocated to Reed Street.) Another general store was A. Hallock's on the main thoroughfare at West Coxsackie. He would advertise he was willing to take telephone orders at 21-4.

Jacob Zimmerman's Ice Cream Parlor and Candy Store on Lower Mansion Street was well patronized by families, courting couples and the neighborhood children, all having a choice of dishes of ice cream or ices but no sodas. Fancy boxes of candy, fruits and nuts were generally available in season. Solicited were quantity orders for weddings, parties and receptions. Fine cigars were a sideline at Antonio Sbarboro's (established in 1887); ice cream, confectionery, fruits and vegetables, and tobacco were also available. Dayton Smith, buying out Frank Worden's establishment, operated a busy News Room on Reed Street. He would also represent the Township on the County Board of

Supervisors.

It was Mike Dolan's heyday as a businessman at the Landing, he making use of the services of his family and also hired help. Of the several Dolan activities, mention is made of the "Boots, Shoes, Hats and Men's Furnishing Store, the house delivery of milk and cream, the availability of wholesale quantities of fresh and salt meats and also poultry. His Central Hotel, mentioned heretofore, was also a dispensary for wine, ales, liquors and cigars.

The Union Liberty Clothing House, Myer Bresky, proprietor - "Gents Furnishing Store - 27 Reed Street" advertised: "No trouble to show goods. Save expenses to Albany." Nearby J. E. Browne, Jr. was acting as agent for Union Laundry and McFarland's Dye Works, his office being with B. S. Hutchings, 18 Reed Street: "Baskets of soiled laundry brought in, laundered at Catskill and picked up at Brownes." For a period of time Coxsackie had a Chinese laundry which provided some competition.

Furniture retailer, undertaker and funeral director, as well as dealer in carpets, oil cloth, window shades and baby carriages brought John Frank a livelihood. He also had skills as a furniture repairer and upholsterer. Advertising solely as a Licensed Embalmer and Undertaker was James H. Lampman at 9 Reed Street. Bereaved families preferring the older "ice chilled" method could be accommodated.

Haircuts were available six days the week at Julius Jerome's on Reed Street. To further enhance his trade, he stressed his membership in Hollister Post No. 27, G. A. R., he being a Civil War veteran. As a member of Coxsackie's Board of Trade, he also wanted patrons to know he was an active participant in civic programs.

Out on Washington Avenue, at his house, N. B. Wagner, offered a broad line of musical instruments and related merchandise. He could be hired to furnish music for all social occasions, being the leader of Wagner's Orchestra.

One of Coxsackie's mainstays was Gabriele Pantaleo ("Gabe"), who first arrived in Coxsackie during the ice season of 1905 to operate a shoe repair concession in the rear of Richtmyer and Sax Men's Clothing store, then located at 3 Reed Street. (Gabe would purchase the firm in 1919.) In after years he often told how difficult it was for him to find reasonable accommodations that first sojourn of 1905, the iceworkers overwhelming local housing space.

Unlike some main streets, Coxsackie never saw any substantial use of paving brick such as that produced at Catskill by the Shale Brick Works. During the wet weather, especially in the spring, complaints concerning "seas of mud" and the need for board crosswalks were ever present. In the dry summer months dusty thoroughfares were the norm. Horse drawn vehicles plus drovers of livestock did little to improve the situation. The use of the Village water sprinkling wagon to "wet down the streets" during the summer months was a boon to both property owners and travelers; it not only reduced the dust but also helped limit the irritants to eyes and noses. Windows and doors could be opened for ventilation, air conditioning being far into the future. One store did have a primitive cooling system — Sbarboro's had fans, pulleys and wheels.

The beginning of the 20th century saw another downtown disaster — the ice gorge formation in the winter of 1901-1902. Piling up between Coxsackie and Stuyvesant Light Station, the ice floes caused the river to back up, flooding many riverfront buildings. When the jam let go the Coxsackie Lighthouse was an early victim, its north wall receiving the brunt of the force. Although heavy foundation stones were displaced, the west wall bulging and cracking, the first floor filling with ice and with holes appearing in the building on the north and the south sides, the tower stood and continued to cast its light. Emergency repairs were completed by June including a new set of lamps. (This repaired structure would function until, in 1940, it was replaced by a metal automatic light skeleton tower and the lighthouse demolished.)

It was during this period of time that toll turnpikes everywhere were succumbing to the public's demands for free highways as voiced by the Good Roads Association as the automobile became a more important means of transportation. The Coxsackie Turnpike corporation had, over the decades, abandoned the less profitable sections of that road. Finally, in 1910, William T. Haswell of Climax, owner and operator, as well as ex- supervisor for the Township, turned over title to the most easterly section to Greene County. To finance this county purchase, on May 1 of that year, county treasurer Judson A. Betts offered six bonds for sale on the new court house front steps. Potential bidders and interested observers, among these being Coxsackie's supervisor, Dayton B. Smith, watched the bidding. The first six bonds were sold at par to Mr. Haswell, the remaining three being bid in by Attorney Bloodgood of Catskill.

On April 1, 1909, George Hubbard had turned over the old stage route to Emory Jackson of Urlton. The following year it was reported Warren Ingalls of Norton Hill had purchased the run from Ray Traver, indicating a continued turnover of ownership. (The first motorized bus run to Albany did not begin until 1916, Henry J. Albright then being the owner-driver. His schedule called for one trip the day.)

The spring season of 1909 saw the Kaaterskill, commanded by Captain Ira Cooper, and the City of Hudson, by Captain Benjamin Huff, Jr., making scheduled stops at Coxsackie. The Storm King, the remains of which may still be seen at low tide on the northerly edge of the river park, was put on the Coxsackie to New York run by the Catskill Evening Line in 1911, mainly to provide fruit growers and shippers with a rapid means of moving farm produce to market. Local apple and pear orchardists were being informed the Storm King had a capacity of 4,000 barrels the trip.

A Chamber of Commerce came in 1910 with twenty-five members; attorney Harry McCurtis served as president. The Village Improvement Society was a special effort of the female contingent, they being especially concerned about adequate waiting rooms equipped with sanitary facilities, sidewalks and crosswalks as well as the public horse trough. Mercantile ownership continued to change as when the James H. Lampman Undertaking Parlor was sold out to William C. Brady of Athens in 1911, with Brady's son, William E. being in charge at Coxsackie. The Copper Trolley Wheel Company located at the West End, reorganized in the summer of 1910, with the business office moved from New York City to Coxsackie.

Village volunteer firemen are credited with yeoman service in fighting several disasters but few exceed the West Coxsackie effort which occurred in 1909. It was an effort which saved much of the West End. Shortly after five p.m. on November 20, fire broke out in the shingle roof of the William Woolford Sales and Exchange stables. Sparks carried by a strong south wind spread the fire so that in forty minutes seven buildings were in ashes. Chief Corey and his men fought continuously, supported by the D.M. Hamilton steamer which was called out. Bucket brigades saved numerous other structures by wetting down roofs. Lost in the catastrophe were: Wm. Woolford's Horse Sales and Stables, Frank Radley's blacksmith shop, the West End Hotel Livery Stables and other outbuildings, William Every's West End Hotel, and two barns near the West Coxsackie school. The origin of the fire could not be determined.

It was the will of Eleanor Van Bergen Heermance (1820-1907) which provided for the establishment of the Heermance Memorial Library which today serves a wide area around Coxsackie. (The first library in the Village was a subscription one. Thomas Brigden Carroll in the 1830's housed a lending library at his printing establishment on Reed Street.) Many families still frowned upon the practice of reading novels, and growing children were forbidden to sit and read during the morning hours while there were home or farm chores to be done.

A few well-to-do Coxsackie families, such as the Bronk-Lampmans, had their own private libraries, many of the volumes being handed down through the generations. For most families, however, a Bible, dictionary and few schoolbooks sufficed.

In connection with the Coxsackie stock-financed Academy (incorporated 1837), a library was established for students, teachers and townspeople known to have contributed a minimum of four books. When the new Union School was opened, it also became the headquarters for this public library of a few hundred volumes.

The Heermance Memorial Library, housed in the Heermance home, operates under a Regents charter dated March 13, 1909. Ella Colgrove was its first librarian while Dr. Andrew Van Slyck presided at the board meetings.

 Climax

Driving out on Route 81 across the flatlands preempted by the first Dutch settlers, one may observe three pre-Revolutionary rubblestone houses on the east side of the Kalkberg. These were originally Vandenberg homesteads. While the earliest Richard Jans Vandenberg house is gone, the 1763 dwelling of his grandson, John R. Vandenberg, survives at the south end of Lovecky Road. A brother-in-law to Judge Leonard Bronk, John R. was one of a small group of influential citizens who established the County of Greene in 1800. Northwesterly on the east slope of the hill is the stone residence of Richard, son of Hendrick Vandenberg. On the north side of Route 81 stands the house built by Peter, son of Richard Vandenberg. This structure eventually came into the possession of the Reverend Henry Ostrander, pastor of the local Reformed Church. As a supplementary source of income, he maintained a private school in this house, tutoring college-bound students in classical studies.

Until Route 81 was cut through the escarpment, it swung around the hill to the south. Here for many years in the twentieth century was Jerry's Inn; it was once the site of another Vandenburg homestead and family burial ground. A portion of the early house may be incorporated in the present structure. Opposite was the Foote Inn, where on December 24, 1796, the Coxsackie Lodge No. 50, F. & A. M. was organized, and here it met until the year 1804. It is said that General Lafayette was entertained here during his triumphal tour of 1824, although there is no substantiation for this.

Around the hill and off in the small flat field stood an ancient grist mill now long gone. The small stream which goes underground at this point was the source of the Village of Coxsackie's first water supply. In 1804 wood pipes were laid below the land's surface to bring water to the Upper Landing. Robert Henry Van Bergen wrote that many a Hudson River sloop filled its water butt from this Climax supply. Except for the difficulty at the hill, it was basically a gravity flow. Sections of the pipe still survive in the Bronck Museum's collection of local artifacts.

At the quarry site, its sheer man-cut walls are readily discernible. That mine of limestone is credited with being the source of supply for some of the blocks utilized to build the Erie Canal locks, work completed in 1825. Beers's *Atlas of Greene County* (1867) still marked it as an active quarry in that year of publication.

Coxsackie, N. Y.

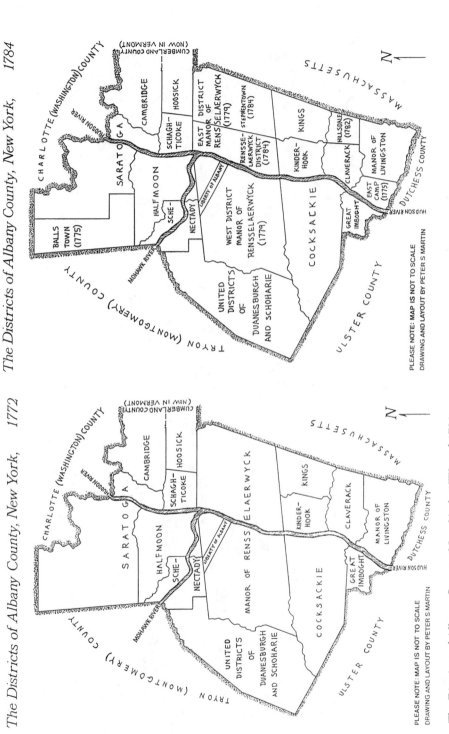

The Districts of Albany County, New York, 1772 and 1784.
Courtesy of The New York Genealogical and Biographical Society. Originally produced in The NYG&B Newsletter.

Reed Street, Coxsackie. (Note the unpaved roadbed and shop walkway shelters.)

Mansion Street, Coxsackie.

The Onteora and Coxsackie at Reed's Landing.

South River Street before the filling-in of the bay.

West Shore R.R. Passenger Station. (Note the Cummings Stage.)

Coxsackie Race Track at the Fair Grounds.

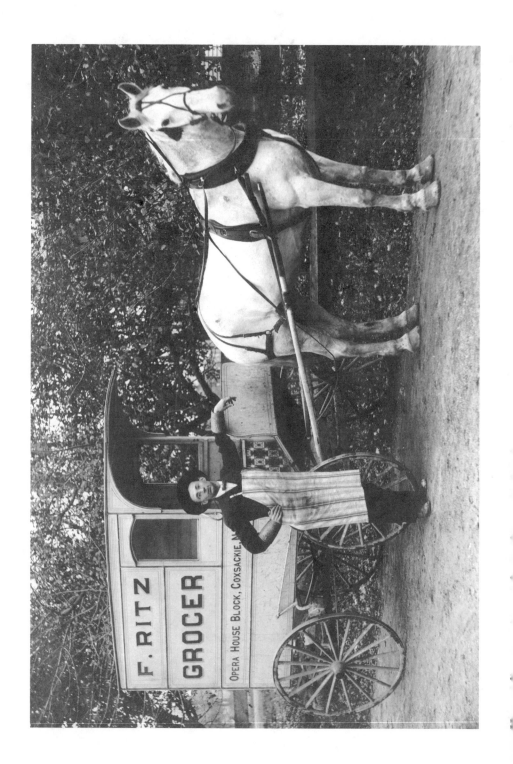

Second Location of Ritz Grocery on Reed Street.

The Ritz Band...

Climax general store and Post Office. (Today's junction of Routes 81 and 26.)

Post Office, Urlton (Earlton).

The fork in the road where Route 26 begins going westerly was long ago the site of a general store. The one-room schoolhouse for this district is now the local post office.

Climax has had four baptismal names. In pre-Revolutionary times this area was known as the Vandenberg Patent and/or the Kalkberg. By early nineteenth century, after the gradual manumission of the blacks, these and other poverty-stricken individuals survived in cabin-like structures on the hill. Colloquially, the name Guinea Hill was then used. Next, in Victorian times, there was an attempt to rename the area Lime Rock. When the postal officials set up a community post office, it was discovered the state already had a Lime Rock; a new name was needed. George H. Scott, the Coxsackie postmaster, is credited with saying to the postal authorities: "We've got a Surprise and a Result, how about a Climax?" And Climax it became!

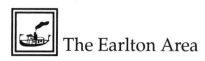 The Earlton Area

Comprised of sections of five patents — Coeymans (1714), Stighkoke (1743), Salisbury (1749), Roseboom (1752) and Scott (1770) — this rural westerly section of the Township of Coxsackie had been virtually unsettled wilderness prior to the close of the American Revolution. It was, however, a prime target for large-scale land speculators. Central to the area is the Stighkoke Patent, a two-mile square section sold by the native owners Herman Backer, Tanighsanow, Aquahannit, Konghan, and Tansaghoes to King George II. Payment was in trade goods valued at 13 pounds 10 shillings. Casparus Bronck, grandson of Pieter and son of Jan, was the negotiator. It was the common practice to wipe out Indian claims but at the same time arranging for title from the Crown's representative in New York. Involved in the purchase, in addition to Casparus Bronck, were Hendrick Remsen, Gerrit Van Bergen and Martin Van Bergen. Their patent is dated June 30, 1743.

For half a century the Stighkoke bounds overlapped that claimed by the Coeymans heirs. It was not until 1768 that, responding to the orders of the Governor and the Provincial Council, the dispute was settled by a survey supervised by the colony's surveyor general and carried out by the assistant, Nanning Visscher. In that land survey, Stighkoke lost its most northerly section.

The earliest settlement in this enlarged Earlton area is credited to one Gerrit Roosa, who had purchased an undivided interest in the Roseboom Patent and had then participated with twelve others in its division by lottery drawing. Roosa also had acquired other acreage in the Stighkoke Patent on which he was, according to Beers's *History of Greene County*, operating a small saw mill "on the south side of the old road east of Earlton." Gerrit Roosa died in 1776 at the outbreak of the Revolutionary War. Both he and his wife, who died in 1787, are buried nearby in the now overgrown fields along Peat Beds Road just before it joins with Route 81.

This section of the Township has small areas of fertile land in narrow valleys and substantial amounts of upland covered with shallow soil. The East and West branches of the Potic Creek, together with smaller runs, provided numerous saw and grist mill sites. Among the earlier operators were Gerrit Roosa, Pazzi Lapham, the Cornwells, the Losees, and Casparus Bronck and partners. The boundary between the Greenville and Coxsackie Townships was moved twice, leaving some Losees first in one political area and then in another.

Pazzi Lapham came from Dutchess County by 1787, purchasing land in the Coeymans Patent on which he constructed his saw mill on the banks of the Potic, also known as Cabin Run. For years this northwesterly section of the Earlton area was known as Lapham Mills. Part of his landholdings would eventually be incorporated in the short-lived Forestville Commonwealth or Community.

Another settler from Dutchess County by 1800 was Henry Cornwell. After he purchased land and established a mill operation on a site previously held by William Sutherland, he continued to expand his operations to the extent that he became one of the most prosperous men in the Township. His surname made Cornwell's Mills another convenient geographical designation. By the close of the nineteenth century, the last of the area Cornwells actively engaged in these commercial activities had passed away. In the year 1899 we find S. P. Hallock, administrator, advertising for the sale of the Cornwell store in the hamlet, together with sheds, barns and nearly two acres of land.

The Forestville Commonwealth at Laphams' Mill was one of the numerous experiments in early nineteenth century communal living inspired and financially assisted by Robert Owen, wealthy English manufacturer. Idealistic in scope, the Forestville Commonwealth collapsed within two years, the land then being sold to John Norbury, James Underhill and John Quinby — all Quakers. Here, in after years, Moses Quinby operated his wood turning mill and also established himself as "Beekeeper to America." Honey Hollow was an appropriate label for that stretch of the Coeymans Patent. One shipment of honey from the Quinby hives and from others nearby was so large in amount, it has been credited with breaking the current market price for that product.

Shadrach Hubbell (Hubble), another pioneer settler, took up land in 1796. One son became an early Earlton schoolmaster, the others relocating in the Village of Coxsackie where they became involved in brickmaking and land development. Another inhabitant was Joseph Bullis, who, in 1799, opened a tavern for the traveling public. His distillery across the roadway was one reason for the local colloquial label affixed to the area, that of "Swill Street."

The 1806 construction of the Coxsackie and Oak Hill Turnpike via today's Route 26 unfortunately did not provide a main thoroughfare for Earlton but rather a branch section linked to Coxsackie. All this was changed with the 1852 building of the Coxsackie and Oak Hill Plank Road, which followed today's Route 81.

The growth of Earlton as a designated community with its own post office is first noted in French's *Gazetteer* (1860.) The use of the name Jacksonville comes from the extensive support of the area's Jacksonian Democrats to the national political organization and to the recognition of Andrew Jackson as a military and political figure. Storekeeper, James F. Burroughs promoted the Jacksonville name in his shipments to and from the hamlet. As time passed, Urlton became the official post office designation, that spelling being changed to Earlton around the time of World War I.

A study of the 1867 Beers's *Atlas of Greene County* (plate eight) indicates the inhabitants of the hamlet and the more rural area were serviced by two general stores: Walter Barlow's on the north (junction of Route 81 and Peat Beds Road) and J. C. Lamphier's across the road on the southeast. In addition to his mercantile operation, Barlow was the proprietor of the Union Hotel. The religious life of the residents at this period of time centered around the Lutheran Church; that edifice was later sponsored by the Methodist Church circuit until its closing in recent years. The hamlet had its own blacksmith shop. In the High Hill area on the West side of the East Branch of the Potic Creek was a flagstone quarry. No record can be found to determine if the local Peat Beds were ever used commercially as a source of fuel as is done in Ireland. All Peat Beds Road is a current recognition of this geological condition.

Beyond Earlton Hamlet, in 1867, was the section of the borderline with the Town of Greenville, a section once known as Pleasant Valley, having its own hotel and store. One of the toll gates for the Coxsackie-Oak Hill Plank Road was located at the western edge of Pleasant Valley.

As farming as a main source of income declined in importance during the latter decades of the last century, many farm families began the practice of taking in summer boarders. By the end of the century those farmhouses were expanded with additional wings and upper stories to accomodate boarders, some even built separate, albeit somewhat primitive, rental cottages. The proprietor's wife frequently did the cooking, assisted by a local hired girl classified as "summer help." The owner generally raised the vegetables and poultry, met boarders at the steamboat landing or train station. A few others arranged for transportation at the ferry terminal. In general, the New York City clientele consisted of families with growing children. July and August were the busy months, school not being in session.

Unlike the more elaborate resorts in the Catskills, these Earlton boarding houses were modest in nature. Rooms were furnished in simple style; plumbing was minimal; weekly rates were low. Guests were expected to entertain themselves with croquet, tennis, bathing in nearby streams, or even with amateur parlor games and theatricals. Hiking along the country roads, generally unpaved, was a pleasant pastime. Dancing was available to live music at Van Hoesen's Hall and later at the relabeled Earlton Country Club. Rifle practice appealed to the male contingent although some braver women were encouraged to fire at targets.

And come for the summer months they did. A local July 31, 1903 newspaper reported: "Boarding houses at Urlton, Result, Gayhead and vicinity are full of guests." Advertising brochures stressed "escape from the city summer heat." One reads in such publications the phrases "well-shaded lawns," "large porches," and "favorable elevation above sea level." By a stretch of the imagination, these boarding houses advertised being "In the foothills of the Catskills." The quality of water from artesian wells was another selling point, as was the "absence of malaria."

Among the larger boarding houses was the Potic Mountain House, an eighth of a mile from the hamlet center. In 1899 this house could comfortably accommodate about twenty guests. After the addition of a third story and other expansion in the early 1920's, that figure increased to seventy-five. At first its proprietor, Malbone W. King, was content to charge $5 the week but with the change in the value of money during World War I, by the early 1920's guests could expect to pay between $16 and $18 the week.

The summer season of 1899 was unusually prosperous for the Urlton resort owners. Charles Woodruff's hotel was housing and feeding twenty paying guests. His clambakes were a novelty both to his boarders and to others. Rylandas Smith's Pine Grove House was a popular place, especially since he had installed a bowling alley. He also featured dancing and evening lawn parties under the Chinese lanterns.

The Urlton Ladies Aid Society frequently scheduled their lawn parties and bazaars during July and August to take advantage of the wallets and pocketbooks of the summer guests. An occasional event was specifically advertised to benefit the pastor, to which the boarders frequently lent their amateur talents.

There had been so many disappointments relating to the Coxsackie and Greenville electric trolley line, that when two canal boats tied up at Coxsackie's lower landing to remove railway ties stored there unused for two years, it seemed to be further conclusive evidence of the impracticality of that transportation idea. But once again, in the summer of 1899, the residents along the route, including the Urltonites, had reason for hope. Not only was Urlton to be a station on the railway line but it was also to be the headquarters for the powerhouse and the car barn! In early December the trolley company purchased the Sylvanus Losee mill property and let contracts for the construction of the powerhouse and the car barn. The fact that William S. Vanderbilt (summer home now the Greenville Arms), as treasurer for the Knickerbocker Trust Company of New York, was active in the line's promotion and financing was another reason to think Urlton would at last be connected by rail to the outer world. In addition to the buildings at Urlton, it was planned to import Italian labor to lay the railway tracks. Shanties were to be built for temporary housing. But these high hopes, like those earlier, were once again subject to disappointment. As funds ran out, construction was halted, never to be resumed. The gasoline- powered automobile provided the final blow to any rural electric trolley line between Coxsackie and Greenville. The future of Urlton lay in small-scale farming, especially hay, fruit and dairy products, with improved roads and the automobile enabling the wage earner to commute.

The Township's Architecture

A wealth of architectural design is observable fronting the various roadways in Coxsackie Township — buildings of stone, brick and wood. The earliest Anglo-Dutch homesteads were established along the windings of the Coxsackie Creek and its tributaries. From the quantity of Indian artifacts found at the various farmstead sites, it is assumed the early settlers took advantage of the cleared tillable plots of ground utilized by Indians. The advantage of a good flow of clear water close by was not to be discounted. Those houses which have survived — the Van Vechten, Bronck, Vandenberg, Van Bergen and Wells — are prime examples of stone structures influenced by the North European building tradition. This continued into the second and third generations. The Spoor house on Murderers Creek is another rural example.

The earliest more urban setting was at West Coxsackie, a small settlement of the King's Road which connected the west side of the Hudson Valley with the lower reaches and into the Jerseys. Its local inland route took advantage of the more level stretches, thus avoiding the steep river banks and cuts. In West Coxsackie, houses were wood framed and simple in style. Some of them were built on glebe lands sold off for the benefit of the First Reformed Church. The Upper Landing also was the site of a few early structures.

By the 1790's investor interest was directed to the commercial prospects forthcoming at the Middle and Lower Landings. Building lots were sold off at a rapid pace after the Bronck and Van Bergen heirs subdivided and sold off portions of their patrimony. Here were built a number of federal units, some influenced by the subsequent Greek Revival style. Few, if any, brick structures along Reed Street predate the 1850's. Periodic fires were a ravager.

As local residents prospered, more elaborate houses were constructed. Abraham Van Dyck's brick two-story addition to the early stone house and John L. Bronk's federal brick residence illustrate the income of the professional class. Dr. John Ely's "first house on the hill" (on Ely Street) is another example. Businessmen such as the Hubbells, Wrights, Mayos, Reeds, Barkers and Heermances have left substantial reminders of their prosperity.

Mansion Street in the Village is a mixture of architectural styles; interspersed are Federal, Victorian, stick carpenter, etc. The Greek Revival house of Henry Greene once graced the site of the old brick school but now is part of an apartment complex on Elm Street. The Union School is Romanesque in style, its front doorway being typical of that school of architecture.

The ravages of fire, neglect and site clearance for newer structures have taken their toll of several notable buildings. Among these are the 1854 brick English Gothic Episcopal Church, the William Mayo Greek Revival House on South River Street, the pre-Revolutionary Bronk dwelling in the fields at West Coxsackie and the second First Reformed Church edifice.

Of the mansion-like brick and wood structures built in the nineteenth century by the related Reed and Fitch families, only two survive — the Gothic brick Fitch residence just south of the Village line on Route 385 and the Reed family's high Gothic-style "Farview" near the Sleepy Hollow development on Route 385. Gone are the Roswell Reed brick structure which stood opposite the family cemetery on Route 385 and the Simeon Fitch homestead at West Coxsackie near the underpass, once operated as the Park Hotel. The Roswell Reed, Jr.-Adams-Grosbeck expanded farmhouse known as Meadow Ridge survives only in the gaunt fire-discolored chimneys.

Ely Farm is a combination of an earlier simple farmstead (north wing) plus a turn-of-the-century addition in the so-termed French chateau roof and porte cochere villa style. It was the main residence of Adelaide Ely Bronk and her husband, the Reverend Lewis Lampman, after his clerical retirement.

Other houses throughout the Township are interesting owing to setting, architectural style or historical associations. Klinkenberg at Four Mile Point, a combination of stone and brick, replaces an earlier structure on the site. It is one of the earliest homesteads on the Loonenburg Patent. The Vosburg, Saunders, Lampman, Kennedy, Tryon and Collier houses all have points of interest. Although over the Town line into New Baltimore, the Van Bergen-Warren Georgian dressed stone residence has many ties with Coxsackie.

There are notable examples of exterior doorways as well as interior woodwork; a few are mentioned. The brick VanSlyke residence on upper Lawrence Avenue, the Hubbell-Van Bergen structure on Ely Street, and the Van Dyck homestead on that named street are all noteworthy examples of fine main doorways. The front and back parlors of the Hubbell-Van Bergen (Adams-Whitbeck) Ely Street structure feature Rams Horn wood trim while the Reed house (corner of New and Ely) has a mantel once coveted by the Metropolitan Museum of Art. The Heermance Memorial Library's mouldings also reflect a woodcarver's skill.

 The Brick Industry

The abundance of suitable clay, nearby supplies of kiln wood as well as cheap water transportation for heavy bulk cargo brought Coxsackie to the forefront of New York's brick industry. By the 1830's at least twenty-five small yards were producing over fifty million bricks the season. Charles Bartlett was among the earlier manufacturers at the Upper Landing. While some yards did manufacture the more expensive face or dress brick, most concentrated on the output of the common variety. Twenty-five sloops hauled this cargo to the metropolitan areas from Coxsackie's various landings. The average run of brick, frequently used and painted in lieu of the more expensive face brick, brought between $3.50 and $5.50 the thousand at New York.

A good workman could earn a minimum of one dollar the day while a man with team could demand two dollars fifty cents. Board or room and board was readily available in Coxsackie, providing houses with a secondary income. Farmers and others owning woodlots with stands of hard wood could depend upon the brickyards to purchase the formers' output.

The demand for brick fluctuated, it being subject to the economic conditions of the time. With Coxsackie brick meriting a higher reputation than some other geographical regions, such producers as Ambrose Baker could also seek out special markets; he secured the contract to supply bricks for the building of the Croton Water Works.

The Panic of 1837 and unforeseen subsequent ones meant financial disaster to several Coxsackie businessmen such as Olney F. Wright, Peter Hubbell, and Edwin N. Hubbell, all of whom made and lost substantial amounts of capital. When the Upper Landing brickyard of Stephen Brown failed in 1869, many creditor merchants suffered heavy losses. The most resilient businessman of all was Peter Hubbell who, after losing out at Coxsackie, eventually relocated to Charleston, Massachusetts. There he became a leading producer of bricks for the Boston market. His utilization of more inventive processes also enhanced his firm's profitability. At the time of his death, he was rated one of Massachusetts' wealthiest men.

A rare glimpse of Coxsackie's brickyard scene in 1835 is contained in a letter in the Reed Adams Memorial Collection, at the Vedder Memorial Library. In that year, on December 25, we find Henry Adams writing to his brother in New York:

I have this morning Rec'd yours of the 21st Inst in which you wish to inquire how many and at what price brick could be procured here on contract. I have seen a number of manufacturers. O. T. Wright has two million bricks on hand, 800,000 of which are front [face] brick. He will take $7.50 and $5.50 [per thousand]. Hallenbeck has 900,000, Vosburgh and Wolfe 500,000, Hubble [Hubbell] has sold his to Bartlett & Van Schaick yesterday at $7 and $5. At the upper landing there are about one million all of which can be got except what is sold, with the privilege of all they make to the first of June or July next — there are about three million at Athens — and a considerable number at Catskill are good brick — as Bartlett and Van Schaick are paying $7 and $5, you will have to pay that or perhaps a little more and must do the same at Athens and Catskill.

Wright is known to have contracted with Mary Shuts at times to board and lodge his brickyard crews of from 12 to 15 men during the season. He was contracted to build a large tenement house at the Upper Landing for a portion of his workmen, possibly African-Americans. Edwin N. Hubbell competed with Olney Wright for the size of operation at Coxsackie. His plans for the 1868 season called for the production of four million bricks, his yard having produced over nine million the previous season. Probably the largest Coxsackie order for brick came to E. N. Hubbell in 1875, his bricks being used for the construction of the famed Hoosac Railroad Tunnel.

The last decade of the nineteenth century saw workmen at the Frederick W. Noble yard at the Upper Landing moving brick to the West Shore freight station for transshipment. Noble also advertised for cord wood for brickyard purposes. The Cooper and Bell yard employed up to thirty-five men. The Fitzgerald operation at the Upper Landing was destroyed by fire on Saturday, September 14, 1895, the work of an arsonist. Barns, sheds, together with supplies of hay, grain, and the firm's wagons were destroyed; the loss was estimated at over $3,000. Blame was assigned to a Hudson brickyard worker with a fancied grievance.

In the summer of 1929, as costs of brickyard operations continued to rise, imported Belgium was being offered for sale for less than the cost of local manufacture. Throughout the Hudson Valley, including the Township of Coxsackie, yard after yard shut down. The final blow was the Panic of 1929, which brought construction to a virtual standstill. Athens yards struggled on for another decade under Mayonne family ownership but finally they also lost out financially and closed down.

Of related interest to Coxsackie's brickmaking is the fact that A. C. Sloan, a Coxsackie carpenter with an inventive mindset, began the production of brick mould forms at his small shop on Hollister Street. He was the grandfather of Alfred P. Sloan, Jr. who would eventually chair the General Motors Corporation. Some portion of the Hubbell brick wealth came back to Coxsackie when his widow, daughter of the Reverend Joseph Prentiss, provided communion silver and the so-called Peter bell for the Episcopal Church on Mansion Street.

Old railroad ties were an inexpensive source of kiln fuel at the turn of the century. Brought in by the barge load, they were quickly unloaded and hauled to the various yards.

While Coxsackie's brick industry was a dying one, the Walsh yards across the river at Stockport were operating at maximum capacity in 1899, producing, it was reported, 350,000 bricks the day during the season. Rumors would have it that the brick trust was acquiring that operation for $200,000 after determining there was enough clay to last for another century.

 Entertainment

Like many upstate rural areas, most of the social entertainment for the community centered around the home, school, church, and local membership clubs. A change came for Coxsackie in the spring of 1870 when Winslow Case opened his 32 x 70 foot entertainment hall in his Reed Street building. To reassure timid patrons, Case publicized the side staircase entrance from the street level to the third floor of his brick block. The room boasted a 12-foot stage with drop curtain painted by C. C. Wells, the local photographer and artist in oils, as well as elaborate chandeliers. Case's New Hall had a "sell out" crowd of between 400 and 500 patrons as Chase's Cornet Band gave an opening evening concert at 8 p.m. on April 29, 1870. Tickets were 25 cents; the doors opened at 7 p.m. to accommodate the crowd.

Hoping to profit financially from the roller skating craze of the 1880's, N. H. Vosburgh, Fred Noble and Dr. A. V. D. Collier contracted for the construction of an indoor rink on Washington Avenue. Operating between 1880 and 1886, under the name of Empire Skating, the youth and more adventuresome adults performed to the music of a local orchestra housed in the balcony. Competition skating included prizes for the fancy waltz as well as racing events. "Dolph" Decker soon earned the reputation of being the "fanciest" skater while William Wells merited the speediest label. A number of Coxsackie males joined the Hudson River Roller Skating League under the restriction that only one professional skater would be permitted on any one team.

The Coxsackie Trotting Track and Fairground was another civic enterprise which came into being in 1883 on land between Mansion and Lafayette Streets. Here numerous trotting and harness racing meets were held on its rail-encircled half mile track. It also served for spur of the moment bicycle races. The Fair site contained stable accommodations for horses, a grand stand for viewing, as well as an exhibition hall for other activities. The Coxsackie Fair Grounds Association also held a yearly agricultural fair each August. The fifteenth such effort was advertised for August 16-18, 1898. Officers responsible for the year's successful event were Alexander Cumming as president, Henry J. Wolfe as vice president, Dr. A. V. D. Collier secretary, and Platt Coonley as treasurer. The superintendency of the fair grounds was delegated to F. F. Bedell. Printed booklets publicized the various horse races for trotters and pacers; the purses ranged from $200 downward. The racing rules of the National

Association governed the trotting events while all running ones were to adhere to the Jockey Club rules. First premiums were awarded for entries in eight categories - 451 prizes in all. The following men had the responsibilities for their categories:

Floral Hall and Ladies' Department - Henry Hartt
Fruits and Vegetables - Robert C. Townsend
Dairy Products - Charles Backus
Implements & Machinery - Lewis Flansburgh
Horses - Peter W. Fox
Cattle - Leonard Rea
Sheep & Swine - Peter Fox
Poultry - Lee Smith

The ladies were encouraged to display their "Domestic Manufactures" which included carpeting, yarn, stockings, gloves and mittens. Quilts had to be entered as silk and velvet, crazy, worsted, log cabin, calico patchwork, cradle, and carpet coverlet. Fancy sewing and embroidery included a wide range of entries: crochet, applique, tatting, silk knitting, silk and worsted. Articles of clothing such as slippers, a chemise, handkerchief, skirt, night dress, lambrequin, suit, and/or fascinator might win a premium. Tidies were another opportunity for the fifty-cent prizes, including one for that lady exhibiting the greatest variety. Entries of plants and bouquets of flowers also were encouraged.

The public was admitted to the Fair Grounds no earlier than 8 a.m. and no later than sundown. Single tickets of admission (one entrance only) was 25 cents the adult; children under 12 might enter for ten cents. For the more affluent, yearly tickets at $1.00 were available for unlimited attendance but were not transferrable.

The grand parade, involving all livestock on exhibit, was set at 10 a.m. the third day and usually secured a large grandstand crowd. All in all, the Fair Committee did its best to attract the entire family. The merchants urged fairgoers to view their goods. To that purpose several advertised in the fair booklet: C. J. Collier & Co., Clark & Hotaling, The J. H. Whitbeck Co., Richtmyer & Sax, Antonio Sbarboro and Union Liberty Clothing House (M. Bresky, prop.). Calvin E. Lord urged fairgoers to shop while in town. Overnight accommodations could be secured at Michael Prendergast's American House (Reed and River), Hotel Royal (Case & Edwards, 21 Reed), Young Mike Prendergast's West End Hotel, Cumming Hotel with Livery attached, the Klondyke House and the Steamboat House (South River).

The more intimate waltz dance, an initial scandal in its early days, had finally become socially acceptable. By the changeover of the century, the Terpsichorean Club was a popular social organization as was the Old Guard Dancing Club.

Whatever chance of success Winslow Case had for his third- floor entertainment hall was defeated by the opening of the Dolan Opera House in that spacious block constructed on South River Street. Over the next several decades it would provide a rental hall with comfortable facilities for traveling shows, school graduation ceremonies, meetings for numerous organizations, church benefits and lastly the motion picture. As early as December, 1891, H. H. Franklin, then secretary of the Farmers' Institute, was urging progressive agriculturists to take advantage of the informative training sessions to be held on January 20 and 21 at Dolan's New Opera House.

There is no indication that any serious operatic performances were ever scheduled at Dolan's except for August J. Van's *St. Elmo* with a cast from the Academy of Music at New York. Generally, light opera was the bill-of-fare with such productions as the New York Comic Opera Company's *The Funny Side of Life*. Reserved seats for special events could be purchased at several stores including Jordan and Marsh, druggists. For such productions as *Human Hearts, a Tale of Arkansas*, the public had to expect to pay 25, 35 or 50 cents for preferred reserved seating. When "Diamond Jack" the medicine man, together with his entourage of 35, performed in the Dolan Opera House in March of 1908, this Indian medicine man was giving away free tickets of admission to sick persons needing his advice and product, a "come on."

One of the largest one-night stands, with a cast of 50 and with special scenery effects, was *Uncle Tom's Cabin*. To publicize this event for the evening of December 14, 1910, a large street parade was organized.

By the end of the first decade of the twentieth century, "moving pictures" were the vogue. Dolan's Opera House was more frequently being referred to as the Coxsackie Theater. Leasing the hall during this period, Mr. Crispell promoted "every evening Biograph subjects," while Richard O'Donnell held forth at the piano to furnish background music. Much depended upon the skill of the projectionist, Mr. Vogel. For the more venturesome, enjoying late hours, the manager promised one dance a week after the moving picture show. Generally, patrons could depend upon a schedule of two shows the evening at 7 and 9; matinee every Saturday and holiday at 3; and a Sunday one at 3:15 p.m.; the theater was closed on Thursdays. In the earliest days the nickel charge made a dent in young people's spending allowances.

At first the films consisted of no more than one or two reels so when the 5-reel western, *A Knight on the Range*, was featured, it was a milestone. (The first World War I government-produced picture entitled *"Pershing's Crusade or Following the Flag to France"* was shown on August 14, 1918.)

For a brief period of time, competition for the Coxsackie Theater surfaced when W. I. Barber opened his Novelty Picture Show. Its life was limited.

 Firemanic

Like other communities, leather fire bucket-brigades were the earliest organized means of fighting fires. Each bucket carried the owner's name and was stored in the household in a spot easily accessible when the warning was given. After the fire, the names on the buckets helped identify owners. Leather was superior to wood and metal buckets, and was easier to pass from person to person.

The first fire engine in use at Coxsackie appears to be the Isabella. In detailing the major conflagration on Reed Street on July 10, 1854, the newspaper reads: "...the old goose-neck hand engine Isabella and scores of men with their fire buckets and pails doing little but to amuse the fire which finally burned itself down to the river." In that major disaster some thirty structures of all sorts went up in flames, buildings sited on both sides of the then narrower Reed Street.

Galvanized by the July, 1854 fire, a public meeting was called to discuss a twenty-foot widening of Reed Street which would require the filling in of a portion of the bay on the north side. The proposal was approved and rebuilding was guided thereby. James Jackson of Albany gained the contracts to construct brick three-story stores for Obadiah Lampman, Benjamin Tryon, Finch and Collier, Lasher and Palmer, and John Welch — all on the north side of Reed Street. To match this activity, Messers William Cochrane, Jr. and M. Parker contracted with Schoonmaker of Athens for a similar brick block on the opposite side of the roadway.

Even with a wider Reed Street and the rebuilding with brick, the fears of another major fire were ever present. To provide improved fire protection became the aim of the leading citizens who commenced the solicitation of funds to build and equip a municipal firehouse. As a result of this effort the Hudson River Engine Company No. 1 was established June 6, 1860. William Martin was designated engineer while J. C. Mackey served as foreman. Mention also is made in earlier histories of a hand pumping engine, the Deluge, acquired at New York, apparently replacing the Isabella.

In 1863, taking advantage of the inability of L. Button & Sons, Waterford manufacturer, to deliver one of their engines to South Carolina, Coxsackie purchased the same for $1,400. That engine is now on display at the Firemen's Museum, Hudson. The first serious challenge to the Hudson River Engine Company No. 1 was the 1864 midsummer fire at the Middle Landing when Mygatt's coal and lumber yard, two hay sheds, a freight house, two phosphate storage buildings, two dwelling houses and a hotel were burned out.

The Kuxakee Engine Company No. 2 came into existence in the year 1871, with an appropriation of $3,500 from a tax levy. In early February that year, after a legal disbandment of twelve days, a new company was formed under the name of the D. M. Hamilton Company No. 2, in honor of this leading citizen. A horse-drawn steamer was purchased, it being housed in a brick engine house still in use on the corner of South River and New Streets. That site cost $850 and the building $2,190. Legal incorporation dates from September 13, 1892.

With the establishment of a second company in 1871, William Kempton Reed was elected chief engineer of the Coxsackie Fire Deparment and Albert Parker his assistant.

Eight years later, in 1879, due to unstable finances, the Village Board took possession of the Hudson River Company's engine. George H. Scott, as the catalyst, undertook to reorganize that company in 1881. Its printed booklet, dated March 1, 1882, gives the fire motto "Able and Willing" and also served to promote order and discipline among its members. Duties of each volunteer fireman including "Attending all meetings of the Company; to repair immediately to the engine on every alarm of fire in the Corporation [Village]; to assist in conveying the same to the fire [providing manpower to pull the engine]; and to remain where it was stationed; to assist in working the same, or to attend to any duty as a fireman to which he may be detailed by any officer in command. Also to provide a uniform and fire hat, when two-thirds of the Company shall so determine."

The dues of the Hudson River Company were set at ten cents the month. Various fines and penalties were specified in the booklet, including one of twenty-five cents for failure to appear when the hose was not used and fifty cents when the hose was used. For leaving the drag (towing) rope, while the engine was in motion, without cause deemed sufficient to the Company, an added penalty of twenty-five cents was to be levied. Five members of the Company were to be detailed by the Foreman each month, as near as possible in the order in which their names appeared on the roll, who were during the time they were detailed, to keep the engine and its mountings well cleaned and in good order and also to do the janitorial chores in the engine house.

The purchase of a horse-drawn hook and ladder engine and its incorporation in 1895 as G. H. Scott Hook and Ladder Company No. 1 were significant events in the history of this company. (Scott's bust is displayed on a marble plinth in the front of the Village building.)

On Friday, April 21, 1882, during mid-afternoon, fire broke out in the stable of Hiram Brown's lumberyard on the river shore. A stiff breeze from the northwest helped spread the flames at a rapid pace. In response to the fire alarm, the steamer of D. M. Hamiliton No. 2 and the hand engine of G. H. Scott were soon fighting the fire, giving special attention to the prevention of the flames spreading down South River Street. Next to burn, after Brown's, was the

Fitchett coal yard containing about 300 tons of that fuel. In the meantime, seeing the wood siding of the Larabee Hotel beginning to blister from the heat of the fire, the crew of the steamship Redfield uncoiled 300 feet of hose and commenced plying that and other nearby buildings with streams of river water.

Even with two fire companies and the Redfield crew's efforts, the flames spread out of control. Two dwellings occupied by the Sherman families were the next to go, to be followed by the Van Loan fishhouse, the Brown lumber yard sheds, the Larabee icehouse, the Sherman grocery store, the express office and shed, plus the Reed and Powell storeroom; badly damaged but saved was their new brick office. As the fire burned out, except for the Fitchett coal piles which burned for four days, estimated damage to buildings and contents surpassed the $31,000 mark; insurance covered $12,000 of the loss. The firms of Brown, of Fitchett and of Sherman had successfully removed their safes ahead of the flames.

Again, on October 20, 1894, the Landing was ravaged by fire; lost were seven storehouses on South River Street owned by the D. M. Hamilton Estate. The Knickberbocker icehouse caught fire but was saved by the efforts of the volunteer companies, as were other scorched structures.

Twenty-five volunteer firemen responded to the fire at the Buffing Wheel factory on Riverside Avenue in August, 1903, thought to have been caused by spontaneous combustion of rags and waste. The D. M. Hamilton steamer fought the blaze by pumping extra water from Dr. Van Slyke's nearby cistern.

West Coxsackie's fire fighting capacity was enhanced with the formation of Coxsackie Hose Company No. 3 on November 30, 1884. Their first piece of apparatus was a four-wheeled horse drawn carriage. Next to be acquired was a two-wheel hose cart. To that company goes the distinction of acquiring Coxsackie's first motorized equipment — a La France hose and chemical engine. Hoping to surprise the attendees at a forthcoming Greene County Fire Convention to be held at Coxsackie, Hose Company No. 3 had two volunteers drive that motorized piece of equipment in from Elmira in time for the convention. The West Coxsackie fire company also sponsored the Earlton Fire Unit in 1964, now an independent company in a modern fire house in that hamlet.

An effort to establish an independent unit in its own fire house at the Upper Landing was underway in 1894. The D. W. Morgan Hose Company No. 4 was the result; it lasted until disbandment in 1913.

Flour, Feed, and Food Processing

The grinding of grain for human and livestock consumption, utilizing water power, is part of the economic history of most pioneer communities. Grist mill sites on good flowing creeks had special monetary values to land developers. Financiers like Roswell Reed of Coxsackie were continuously involved in such site speculations. With the development of steam powered processes, owners and manufacturers could site their mills and food processing plants without concern for mill ponds and water flow. It also meant a much more dependable source of grinding capacity.

The Bronck and the Van Bergen families were among the earliest to secure at least a portion of their incomes from grist mills. Others came to be owned and operated by the Titus, Powell, Hallock and Dean families. The Coxsackie mills, during the Revolutionary War, were an important source of supply to feed the troops and otherwise sustain dwellers in the war-ravaged areas.

Most of the small mill operations came under intense competition after the opening of the Erie Canal in 1825 and the rapid development of flouring mills in central and western New York. As a result, quality white flour declined as a local grist mill product, although other grains such as buckwheat and rye continued to be ground. A few of the mills also processed a plaster from limestone.

Destroyed by fire in 1896, the Van Bergen mill on the Coxsackie Creek just over the town line into New Baltimore had ground farmers' grain since the first quarter of the eighteenth century. Here also was produced ground lime. In 1883 Nelson and Henry Van Bergen would open a steam-powered mill at West Coxsackie, they had purchased the old Reformed Church parsonage for that purpose. Like the other mills, it was a victim of changing times in the twentieth century.

Hallock's Steam Mill (today's Betke Street area) was both a feed and plaster mill, built about 1870. Employed here were five men on a regular basis. Powered by a 20-horsepower engine, the Hallock mill processed 15,000 barrels of grain and 300 tons of plaster ingredients annually.

The Titus Flouring Mills, situated 2 1/2 miles west of Coxsackie, eventually came under the control of the Van Bergen brothers. In March of 1870 Robert Henry Van Bergen advertised a lease or sale of the Titus Mills and their 40-acre site.

In more recent years the Hood family maintained a feed operation at West Coxsackie. Over the years this site close to the West Shore Railroad tracks had several advantages over other mills, especially for livestock feed.

In the early years of the nineteenth century, Titcomb the baker had a modest cracker manufactory at the Upper Landing. Except for Robert Henry Van Bergen's *Ye Olden Time*, no other mention of this enterprise can be found.

Food processing on a larger scale was a source of seasonal income in Coxsackie, especially for females. A Mr. Philips from St. Lawrence County, associated with Coxsackians Isaac Mygatt and Levi Bedell in the spring of 1882 to purchase land on Mansion Street next to the old cemetery on which to build a plant for the steam drying of fruit. Plans called for a work force of from 20 to 30 women and also a few men, for about four months the year.

The canning of sweet corn, peas, apples and occasionally other farm products was the specialty of E. H. Lounsberry of Coxsackie and Joseph F. Brown of Poughkeepsie. Operating under the name of E. H. Lounsberry & Co., their processing plant on Mansion Street was a source of employment for between 50 and 80 persons during the harvest months. The females husked the corn, shelled the peas and prepared the apples, the men operated the machinery. Hand labor gave way to machine as the operation got underway. It was the policy of this firm to contract each spring with local growers, thus insuring an adequate supply of produce if the weather cooperated. For the 1886 season contracts were signed for 140 acres of corn and 100,000 cans were stocked. By midsummer E. H. Lounsberry & Co. was processing 1,400 daily. In mid-September, 1891, ten tons of corn came down on the boat from Coeymans.

The 1897 season saw a shortage of sweet corn from surrounding farms so the canning factory turned to apples to take up the slack. The firm was hoping to process between 20,000 and 30,000 one-gallon tins. When corn was available, it was cut from the cob and the cans filled by specialized machinery, thus reducing the amount of hand labor required. The summer of 1900 saw the installation of a new piece of machinery - the pea podder.

Brand names promoted by the E. H. Lounsberry & Co. firm included Little Gem, Rip Van Winkle, and Greene County. These were well-regarded by the wholesale trade. The gallon-size cans were in demand for restaurants, boarding houses and institutional kitchens.

Cold storage for apples and pears was another means of making fruit available during the off season. In August, 1900, Winans and Bailey were buying up the pear crop for their insulated warehouse. Cold storage plants continued in operation for many years, one of the last being Carey's at West Coxsackie.

Van Wie and Delamater in the 1897 season were hiring 24 females and 15 men to operate their 8 apple paring machines and 3 drying kilns. Tons of apples were being processed on a daily basis, it being their practice to prepare the fruit and fill the kilns by day, permitting the apples to dry at night. Delamater eventually became the sole proprietor but lost out in 1910 when the building was struck by lightning and burned.

During this era, P. W. Fox at his West Coxsackie cider mill (formerly D. Youman's) was in the market for about 50 barrels of apples the day.

The West Coxsackie Creamery was a new enterprise in 1897, utilizing what was termed a "Russian separator" to process cream and also help in the churning of butter. This separator had a capacity of 2,000 pounds of milk the hour, while churning equipment could produce 120 pounds of butter every other day. As a dairy operation it had limited success, there being turnover of operators, the Smith Dairy of New York being one. Levi Garrett was their butter maker.

The shipment of apples and pears from area orchards created a need for shipping containers — barrels of sufficient strength to stand rough handling to places as far away as to Europe. Established at Reeds Landing on South River Street in 1874, T. B. Alcott's barrel manufactory could meet a demand of 60,000 barrels the year. In addition to a seasonal payroll of between 10 and 12 men, Alcott's was a steady purchaser of barrel staves from area farmers. This industry continued to expand, Coxsackie having five such cooperages at the turn of the century. Many barrels were shipped elsewhere which was one reason Alcott first located on the river front, having his own wharf.

A skilled cooper could make an excellent wage. By 1900 he could earn 5 cents the barrel for "setting up" and 20 cents for each assembly. A skilled workman might produce 100 barrels the working day, thus earning $25.

There were years when local growers of fruit complained the commission merchants at New York, or their counterparts, were the only ones profiting. Soft fruit such as strawberries and raspberries, and grapes, had to be moved to market rapidly. Firmer fruit such as apples and pears could be held in cold storage hoping for a higher price in the off season. Risk was ever present as when meadow moles undermined the floor of the Charles H. Delamater cold storage building, thus destroying the ice effect. But even the barrel producers had to assume some risks. One Reeds Landing flood found the Alcott employees doing their best to salvage 50,000 staves in danger of floating away.

Freight Forwarding and Passenger Service

Transportation across the Hudson River for passengers and light freight was available between Coxsackie and Newton Hook for all of the nineteenth century and well into the twentieth. The opening of the Rip Van Winkle at Catskill bridge diverted many patrons; rising cost of operation also was a contributing factor to the ferry's demise. Advertised as the shortest crossing between New York and Albany, the privately owned, monopoly franchised ferry company at Coxsackie had a history of frequent change in ownership and noticeable lack of adequate profits. Municipal operation was proposed in the final years.

Until the growth at Reeds Landing, the cross river ferry service was provided by Ephraim Bogardus at the Upper Landing. Undoubtedly there was some limited private transportation available for hire before 1800 but it was in that first year of the new century that Bogardus successfully sought and secured a monopoly grant for a ferry at Coxsackie. His schedule of rates, like the toll roads, was subject to the oversight of the Court of Common Pleas. Isaac Wells and his son continued the early ferry operation with a scow powered by sail, or in calm weather, by oars.

Seeing the potential for a more profitable run from the Middle Landing, in 1820 William Judson, Andrew Whitbeck and John L. Sharp applied for and were granted a monopoly franchise for a term of twelve years subject to renewal privileges. It was the goal of this new corporation at Reeds Landing to provide a more dependable crossing service than heretofore offered by sail and manpower. To that purpose, the new firm contracted with Goodrich's shipyard for a modern mechanical boat — a horse powered treadmill scow. Tunis Cochran had a major part in its building, he being a local craftsman with considerable skills.

The Judson and Sharp interests held control for approximately fifteen years during which time they either operated the ferry boat themselves or else leased the operation. The ferry stairs (wharf) was improved, and in 1834 a new horse ferry was on the ways of the Mayo shipyard, the latter having been taken over from Goodrich.

Eight years later, in 1842, the Judsons and related partners sold out to George Reed, Silas Holbrook and Attorney Peter H. Silvester. These men had assured the state officials they were prepared to put a new ferry boat into service should the charter be renewed for another twelve years. With favorable state reaction, the William Mayo shipyard constructed the horse ferry christened the William V. B. Heermance (William Van Bergen Heermance, founder of the Coxsackie Bank). It is believed this vessel was eventually converted to steam operation; it saw continued service between Coxsackie and Newton Hook until the delivery of the Coxsackie in 1878. That vessel had been constructed at New Baltimore by the Baldwin firm, the Coxsackie shipyard being closed down. By this date the William H. Thomas family had assumed operating control; their relationship with the Coxsackie Ferry continued for several decades.

Closely connected with the Coxsackie Ferry Company for a period of time was David Miller Hamilton who was also actively involved in freight forwarding at the Landing. At the time of his death in 1892 he was listed as the managing owner.

The Coxsackie Ferry was always good for a news item or two. For instance, in August, 1910, the public was being notified by the editor to be cautious, as the newly installed safety valve on the ferry might scare any horses waiting on nearby Reed and Powell dock.

The trio of landings on the navigable Hudson at Coxsackie was ideal for the handling of both incoming and outgoing freight and passengers. For more than a century and a half warehouses existed at the docks. With the opening of the Coxsackie Turnpike out to Greenville and beyond, as well as the north-south Albany and Greene Turnpike, both in the first decade of the 19th century, these traffic arteries provided main land routes for the movement of raw materials and manufactured goods.

Baker & Company was one of the earliest freight forwarding firms, its location at the Upper Landing enhanced that firm's ability to supply pure water for the sailing sloop butts. At West Coxsackie the McVickar Brothers had a multiple trading operation and also sailed their sloop Morning Star to and from New York. Archibald and James McVickar prospered enough to build a new store in 1802. Its river commerce grew so rapidly that by late August of 1804, it had already made twelve trips to metropolitan New York for that season. It is believed the Morning Star, a vessel of seventy-six tons burthen, had been rebuilt in 1801 in a Coxsackie shipyard.

The successful effort of Reed to develop the Middle Landing which soon carried the family surname, brought about the gradual decline of the Upper Landing. The removal of the ferry operation to Reed Street and the failure of Baker & Company were added factors enhancing the Middle Landing growth. Here, over the decades, Baker and Kirtland, Hamilton and Smith, Barker and Judson, Smith and Van Schaack, the Farmers' Freighting Company, as well as the Reed and Powell Transportation Company were among the more active freight agents.

Baker, Kirtland & Company transported both passengers and freight. In the spring of 1837 they put their new barge The Farmer on the Hudson to begin service April 1. This firm also purchased the steam vessel New Castle for passenger runs.

Farmers came to feel they could profit more adequately if they could eliminate the local commission merchants and freight forwarders. In 1836 at the Lower Landing these agriculturists formed the Farmers' Freighting Company. Among the $500 share holders were Aaron Butler, Obadiah King, R. Edget, David Webber and I. W. Lampman. One of their first moves was to purchase the barge Fishkill and employ Captain Halstead. This freighting concern operated for two years but had limited success. It was then sold to Captain Isaac Smith and Benjamin Burroughs, operating under the name of Smith and Van Schaack.

David Miller Hamilton, coming from Greenville at the age of 19 years, first gained employment with the freighting firm of Smith and Van Schaack. After marriage to Captain Smith's daughter in 1863, he and his brother-in-law expanded that firm's operation. In 1872 the Lower Landing dock was acquired by Hamilton and Smith with plans to once again resume freight forwarding. The new firm met a temporary set back that year when their propeller vessel McManus burned to the water's edge while lying at the dock at the foot of Franklin Street, New York; fortunately the crew escaped a sudden death.

The Thomas McManus, then captained by S. R. Carrol, had been leaving Coxsackie every Tuesday and Thursday at 3:30 p.m. Its usual schedule called for stops at Hudson Landing, leaving that city for New York at 7 p.m. Those desiring to travel upriver could depend upon the Monday, Wednesday and Friday runs with a 6 p.m. cast-off at New York. David M. Hamilton stressed his Coxsackie and New York Steam Freight and Passenger Line's connections with the Medway, Greenville and Medusa stage and also with the City of Hudson steamer for those desiring to reach Stuyvesant, New Baltimore, Coeymans, Castleton or Albany.

The Coxsackie, Albany and Newburg Day Boat Line's Jacob H. Tremper provided connections upriver for Albany and intermediate landings every Monday, Wednesday and Friday at 1:45 p.m. The downriver run in the year of 1872 included a stop off at Coxsackie at 10 a.m. Alternating days with Captain T. Scott Millegan of the Tremper was the M. Martin commanded by Captain Zach Roosa. Both captains were prepared to give "Particular attention to the delivery of orders, purchasing of goods, or business commissions of any description."

The Reed and Powell Transportation Company's office and warehouses were in a strategic location overlooking Reed Street and the river wharfs. They had purchased the old W. C. Redfield steam vessel at the closing of the White Elephant Railroad. On their Coxsackie dock about 1872, "Quaker John" Powell maintained his windmill, a noted landmark and attention getter. As general commission merchants and forwarders, Reed and Powell moved grain, hay, straw, fruit and all kinds of vegetables.

The driving of livestock from "out back" to the Landings for shipment to New York was a long-standing practice of drovers. It is said the main reason for so many picket fences along Mansion and Ely Streets in the 19th century was for yard protection. At late as 1902 the local press was reporting "several drovers of sheep came through this week from out back for the New York markets."

Down the years until the automobile became the major means of transportation, Coxsackie was included in river line freight and passenger service. Vessels like the steamer Eloise, in 1889, attempted to maintain a regular run between Coxsackie, Hudson and Catskill. The day and night lines also sought a modicum of business from Coxsackie, adjusting schedules to get maximum income. But the river runs for freight and passenger service were a dying operation and as operating costs increased, the Coxsackie stop-offs were eliminated.

 Light Industry

Many upstate Chamber of Commerce committees in the last decade of the 19th century and down to the present time, have sought to induce manufacturers and distributors to utilize empty factory buildings. In some cases special tax inducements and low interest loans are an added offer. Coxsackie has been no exception. In July of 1892, the Board of Trade signed an agreement with J. H. Osterhoudt of Troy to operate a shirt factory here, he being a manufacturer of the well-known Troy Standard shirt brand. Collars and cuffs, then detachable, would be a sideline.

Earlier, the Coxsackie businessmen had purchased a plot of ground near Dr. Van Slyke's residence on Riverside Avenue for such a factory. This 75-foot lot on the street extended westerly 222 feet and was part of the defunct Winslow Case brickyard. For several days after the agreement's completion, carpenter Lee Smith and helpers were busy tearing down the old brickyard's flimsy structures. Next Brown and Tiel would construct the factory building with funds raised by public subscription. While Winslow Case sold this site at a very low price, he hoped to benefit by subdividing the remaining land into residential building lots.

Like many of these firms that had little of their own capital tied up, J. H. Osterhoudt found himself free to leave after a three-year period. Smith & Gary soon began a similar output, only to be burned out.

The Miller-Hale Shirt and Collar Company began in temporary quarters at Reeds Landing, giving employment to a number of local residents, especially females. For many families it was a supplemental income. The tempo of business for this firm was such that it soon began contemplating a modern factory by the Larabee House and ferry slip, the J. W. O'Connor barn to be demolished. Difficulties soon arose connected with the inability to secure clear title and in the end Miller-Hale went to Riverside Avenue. The new building was to be a two-story 50 x 50 foot structure, and would include a basement. The officers of the firm, after letting the contract to John Brown, announced they anticipated the building's use by September 1. Actually they were optimistic by only a few weeks. To raise additional capital for expansion the capital stock of the Miller-Hale Shirt and Collar Company was increased from $25,000 to $100,000. Purchases of cloth were substantial and indicate a large volume of output. One order of muslin in early December of 1899 totaled six tons.

It would not be Coxsackie's only shirt factory. Eventually the old brick church structure on Ely Street would have a similar use.

 Ice Industry

It was a gamble, but with the unexpected opening of the Hudson River in the mid-winter of 1828, and alert to the shortage of ice at New York, Captain Alanson Warden of the sloop Ancona seized the opportunity. His cargo of ice that February brought $300 at the Battery.

The idea of harvesting river ice during the colder months and storing it for the demands of summer is credited to Hiram Van Steenberg of Catskill. In partnership with Charles Backus of Coxsackie and W. Radford, a wealthy city merchant, Captain Isaac Smith's empty warehouses at Coxsackie's Lower Landing were rented and filled with Hudson River ice, hoisted into the wood structures by draft horses. It was a crude but effective operation. Van Steenbergh's obituary (1894) mentions this involvement and credits him with the invention of the endless chain ice hoist apparatus.

With the success of the Van Steenberg-Backus-Radford effort of 1850, others rapidly followed suit. Buildings especially designed for the insulated storage of ice were rapidly constructed on river islands, along the shoreline, and up the larger creeks. The Knickerbocker Ice Company located its first Coxsackie facility at the Lower Landing in 1857; it had a capacity of 30,000 tons. A year earlier, in 1856, the New York and Brooklyn Ice Company employed between 200 and 300 men to fill its eight houses at Athens while William Mayo of Coxsackie constructed two ice barges on his shipyard ways. Joseph Sherman, Tunis Chaddon and Edward Ely Sherman were this era's pioneers in the wholesale ice trade at the hamlet of New Baltimore.

In 1867 the Knickerbocker Ice Company was tearing down its two icehouses at Coxsackie's Lower Landing to be replaced by three more efficient structures powered with steam. At the same time their docks were enlarged. This construction so impressed the *Coxsackie News* that it declared "Coxsackie is the best place on the river to procure ice."

Messers G. Lusk and H. Van Steenbergh purchased Haneverplatt in 1874, an island of about 75 acres with a river frontage of over 1,000 feet. To be constructed thereon was a mammoth ice house.

Coxsackie rapidly became the center of the Hudson River ice trade, with the Knickerbocker ice tows being made up here in 1875. The demand at New York for river ice seemed insatiable. It is estimated that at the conclusion of the 1870 season in March, ice tickets with a face value of over $7,000 had been exchanged by companies for men's labor. These tickets circulated with merchants on an equal basis with cash.

Labor unrest always spread rapidly from one ice field to another, generally at the beginning of the ice season. Coxsackie was the center of labor strife in January of 1872, the crews here striking for the higher wage of two dollars the day. This strike was being watched by all the owners since no ice cutting had commenced anywhere else and the wage rate agreed upon would regulate the scale of wages for the winter. Some owners were threatening to use strikebreakers.

By 1884, from the Brewer House at Four Mile Point to the National House on Rattlesnake Island, the 15 ice buildings had a storage capacity of 401,000 tons. The Knickerbocker Ice Company continued its expansion with the 1892 purchase of the property of the New Coxsackie Ice Company, also known as the Noble Icehouse - capacity of 18,000 tons. Still construction continued! TenBroeck Van Orden of Catskill in September, 1897, was drilling and blasting for the Thomas Bell house north of Four Mile Point (Beecher Road). In February of 1901 Adelaide Bronk Lampman sold to Daniel Geroe Greene and Frank Frisbee Bedell acreage at the Lower Landing for $5,000. Here the two partners contracted with Edward S. Anthony to build a 50,000-ton ice storage house. Work began in September, 1901, and by early February, 1902, the new building was being filled with ice. It was a modern structure in every respect, with electric power, and electric lighting for night work. Each of the three elevators had a 20 horsepower electric motor attached to raise the ice into the building.

The winter ice work, although not the easiest, provided secondary benefits for Coxsackie and inland communities. It meant a supplemental income for heads of families and single men. Those who did not commute on a daily basis sought lodgings in the cheaper hotels and in private houses. Some like John N. Briggs of Coeymans, master mechanic, had steady employment with the larger corporations. He would eventually supervise all mechanical work for the American Ice Company, from Maine to Washington. Store merchants sold quantities of gloves, mittens, caps, heavy underwear, overshirts, working pants and footgear. Restaurants provided hot meals for transient workers and occasionally filled orders for large insulated containers of coffee to be delivered to the ice fields. Business was brisk during the evening hours when the fields were not being worked. As late as February 2, 1912, the newspaper was reporting very quiet days but busy evenings with hundreds of men and dozens of teams making a lively street scene.

While many of the larger ice houses had their own crews, several owners contracted for the filling of their buildings and the emptying of the same. John T. Welch was known to have had his crew fill the Bell Ice House one winter. As one of the more progressive ice merchants he was then residing in the old Fitch Gothic brick mansion at the southern edge of the village. He and his brother had an interest in at least four ice houses but the one easterly of his residence claimed the major share of his time. Known as the Klondyke, presumably from the Gold Rush episode of the time, he soon found enough profit to expand. Welch was always good for a news item such as in the paper of April 13, 1899: "John T. Welch has moved the last of his ice stack at the Klondyke house. He had six boatloads. No more will be taken from there at present, but one of his Catskill houses will be opened. Mr. Welch is making preparation to put a 20,000 ton addition to the north side of his building, to be ready for the next harvest."

Fire was long the bane of the ice industry, the rough framed structures being especially dry when empty. They were tempting summer targets for lightning and could even be fired by disgruntled employees. The adjacent boarding houses, storehouses, workshops and stables were equally vulnerable. Instances of such conflagrations are numerous. In December, 1908, on a late Tuesday afternoon, Brewers House at Four Mile Point went up in a spectacular fire. Consumed in the flames were the ice house itself, a residential cottage, the workshop and storehouse plus all the ice harvesting equipment — a major economic loss. The stables and the boarding house alone survived.

No history of the latter years of the ice industry at Coxsackie and nearby points would be complete without a mention of Robert LeFurgy. It was his practice to employ local crews and move from house to house to process ice as well as to make repairs. The wage scale in 1914 was two dollars the day for the laborers and two dollars and fifty cents for the field boss; the driver and his team could earn as much as five dollars. By 1919 the general ice laborer was earning $4.50 the day. One large ice company found it economically feasible to put LeFurgy on its steady payroll both to harvest ice and in the warmer months to load the ice boats for shipment to New York. When not engaged in ice work, Robert LeFurgy and his crew could earn four dollars the day constructing new ice runs at his shop at 115 South River Street. For a time he also was elected Village mayor.

The use of horsepower was still a common practice. The larger companies frequently shipped horses upriver, each being given its own identification number. Oats and bran were ordered from H. E. Hood & Sons feed mill at West Coxsackie while hay came from several sources including the Welch farm. Veterinarians such as Dr. Parker of Catskill responded to sick and injured horses. John Neary, blacksmith, shod as many as twelve horses in a day for LeFurgy (ice shoes). J. Buddleston was a good man for horses' teeth; he charged one dollar the mouth.

As indoor plumbing developed, with sewage treatment plants being almost nonexistent, the more affluent city dwellers sought ice harvested on inland lakes or from Maine rivers. The average housewife, however, was still more concerned with the zinc lined icebox and the overflow pan than with such environmental matters. The Greene County newspapers did not recognize the health problem from polluted Hudson River ice but rather in January of 1907 were blaming the New York City Merchants' Association, more generally known as the Ice Trust, for a deep conspiracy to discourage the harvesting of Hudson River ice by the smaller companies in order to drive up the price. The Ice Trust in contacting the State Health Commissioner pointed out that many ice houses were situated just below Albany where the river was so contaminated with the sewage of Albany, Troy and other towns as to be absolutely filthy. They warned: "A piece of ice to cool water might contain enough bacteria to decimate an army."

These dire health warnings notwithstanding, the ice harvesting at Coxsackie and elsewhere along the Hudson continued. On January 1, 1915, the *Coxsackie Union* was reporting: "The general ice harvest prospects hereabouts are rather discouraging. The Morse steamboat performance kept the ice breaking and piling up and the water rolled [roiled?], and most of the large fields were ruined before they stopped. It is the same all along the river, and ice getting will be difficult. The Welch house has a good field and will probably be able to fill. Greene and Bedell can get none. The lower landing Knickerbocker can get about 20,000 tons. No ice for the Noble, Dover Platt or Rattlesnake houses on the islands; and the outlook for the Newton Hook house is poor. Work will commence at the Rea house next Monday and there will be enuf [sic] to fill it. Gorman can get about 8,000 tons on the inside of the island, but none outside. Anthony will probably fill up. The Scheumann house at Stuyvesant will be able to fill. The Scott house on Bronk's Island has a good field on the east side of the river. It is hard telling what the conditions may be later, whether better or worse, but at present the ice averages only about 8 inches except where it has been tapped."

Of additional interest in 1915, it was noted that Mr. Gates was filling the Reed and Powell ice house from in front of their dock and he was also planning to fill the McClure and Jordan drugstore one. Will Perry was filling the Cobblestone Inn ice house. The Village ice man, E. W. Smith, was preparing to take in ice at the Lower Landing to serve his Coxsackie customers during the summer; the ice there in his field was between 9 and 10 inches thickness.

It was not the purer lake and Maine river ice which finished off the Hudson River icehouses, rather it was the growth of commercial artificial ice plants and the affordability of the household refrigerator. Slowly Coxsackie's big structures disappeared — some from neglect, some for their lumber, while a few were converted to the growing of mushrooms. Occasionally the local newspaper would carry a news item of another disappearance as on August 29, 1919 when it noted: "Last Saturday the foundation gave way under the Charles Gorman 24-thousand ton ice house opposite the island. The whole building is a heap of ruins. It was the old Greene County ice house up to 40 years ago."

The last ice house structure to survive, the Bedell and Greene, finally owned by the Knaust Mushroom firm, went up in smoke in a spectacular fire in August, 1962. The heated air currents were so intense they carried large chunks of burned wood as far south as the Four Mile Point area. The author's lawn was littered with pieces between one and two feet in length.

 The Metal Foundries

Continuing to serve as a trading and shipping center, Coxsackie and West Coxsackie witnessed substantial growth in the decades following the Civil War. While shipbuilding declined in importance as a source of employment its place was taken by the ice industry and the metal foundries.

In 1866 two such foundries were attracted to Coxsackie, beginning a local industrial pattern which would continue for several decades. With the growth in importance of the steam engine, small industries were no longer dependent on power from the flow of water. Compared to their earlier inland locations, Coxsackie had several advantages. The Hudson River proved a cheap means of transportation for the importation of coal, pig and scrap iron while manufactured goods could be directed to metropolitan centers with little or no trouble. Moulding sand for the casting processes was a local product. The labor supply, including Irish immigrants, was plentiful.

The Coxsackie and Malleable Grey Iron Company was a transplant from Oak Hill. It had been established at that village in 1833 by Adams and Throp to take advantage of a good supply of waterpower. Suffering a major loss from fire, the concern and its Coxsackie investors decided to relocate and build a new foundry. That same year Alonzo Newbury removed from Windham to South River Street. Just why the stockholders of the Coxsackie Malleable and Grey Iron Company selected a foundry site halfway up Mansion Street hill is uncertain. Cheap land? An exchange of land for stock? The location involved a heavy haul from the river docks by teams of horses and wagons, but locate there they did.

Five years later, the Malleable and Grey Iron Works fell victim to fire, the damage amounting to the substantial sum of $50,000. A stock issuance, approved April 17, 1872, financed the brick foundry building, offices, etc. The firm continued to manufacture iron castings and fittings, using an average of 300 tons of pig iron the year. The officers and financial backers were Messers Greene, Dwight, Parker and Mygatt, the latter serving as plant superintendent. The labor force numbered about 75 men. Only marginally profitable in 1885 the firm sold out to Alonzo Newbury who had turned over his South River Street foundry to his brother, Bolivar, in 1881.

Prior to coming to Coxsackie and South River Street, Alonzo Newbury, his brother Bolivar, and the former's two sons had first been involved in foundry work at Red Falls, east of Prattsville. In 1856, the two older Newbury brothers joined with Burton G. Morss in setting up a foundry in the then closed Macomber, Hunt and Olney paper mill in Windham. Here was produced the patented Newbury Printing Press, an Alonzo inventory. This press owing to its small size and low cost became very popular for small print shops both here and in Central and South America. They also produced the Continental model which attracted printers at a distance to the use of that machine.

The Newbury Foundry and Machine Shop on South River Street continued for several decades. It is uncertain why Alonzo eventually withdrew in 1881, leaving its operation to his brother Bolivar. The firm continued to produce the Newbury Printing Press and also a patented paper cutter. Eventually succeeding to the foundry's operation, Alonzo's son James G. became noted as a highly skilled machinist and foundry man. The other Alonzo son, Jay Herbert, in early adulthood was enticed to Pennsylvania for the high wages paid at the Scranton Locomotive Works; he eventually returned to Coxsackie and was employed as foreman of the Malleable and Grey Iron Works. He made two more moves as the decades passed, first joining with a brother-in-law in the operation of a machine shop in Guilderland, Albany County, and finally following his father to Monroe, New York.

From 1855 until Alonzo Newbury sold out the mid-Mansion Street foundry to Albert C. Hotaling, he produced steam fittings and castings. Orders for the printing press continued to come in but the press itself was becoming outmoded for the modern print shops in the United States. As profits continued to elude Hotaling, he also put the Mansion Street site up for sale. The Kennedy Valve Company with its main office at 57 Beekman Street, New York City, was induced to utilize this Coxsackie foundry by local businessmen. The site was purchased with Coxsackie money and lent rent free for ten years.

During the last decade of the 19th century Kennedy Valve provided steady employment for approximately 100 wage earners. First capitalized at $150,000, its assets grew rapidly to over $200,000, and all with limited debt. It has been stated that the firm's shrewd purchasing of railroad carlots of copper ingots for a well-planned manufacturing schedule geared to meet the market's demands enhanced the corporations's profitability. The eventual removal of this firm to Elmira was allegedly occasioned by its inability to secure adequate railroad siding linked to the West Shore's main tracks. Elmira is said to have offered financial inducements for expansion not forthcoming from Coxsackie. In the Elmira move, Coxsackie lost about 100 families when the male wage earners accepted the firm's offer of employment at Elmira.

With foundry work still in his blood after his sale of the Mansion Street site to Hotaling, Alonzo Newbury, after a passage of time, established himself in a new plant at West Coxsackie beyond the freight station. The railroad was taking the place of the Hudson River and Newbury saw advantages at West Coxsackie.

Shortly after midnight on October 13, 1899, Alonzo Newbury's West Coxsackie foundry went up in flames. It had been a busy summer and fall with unfilled orders piling up. The work crew of 22 were now unemployed. Saved from the conflagration were a few special lathes and casting patterns. While the insurance claims were being settled ($10,000 loss; $5,000 insurance), Alonzo and a few workmen filled uncompleted orders at his son's shop on South River Street. Finally he and his family departed for Monroe, New York, a location on the Erie Railroad and closer to Metropolitan New York.

Of the two older generations of Newburys, only James G. remained in Coxsackie processing such specialty orders as 40 tons of beef hangers for the military, which he shipped to Manila on government contract in 1899. It was James G. who sold a section of his South River Street frontage on the Hudson to the new foundry, the American Valve. By the turn of the century, these various foundries were importing quantities of scrap iron. For example, the scow Harold of Rondout unloaded 75 tons of scrap iron at the Coxsackie waterfront in late October, 1899. Locating in temporary quarters built for the Coxsackie Electric Light and Power Company, South River Street, the American Valve in 1900 began the manufacture of brass and iron gate valves as well as fire hydrants. The Newbury foundry next door also was utilized on a temporary basis. American Valve was capitalized by local businessmen at $50,000. Four patents developed by Messers. Whitman and Weller, former pattern maker and draughtsman at Kennedy Valve, were the sources of American Valve's initial success. Conveniently located to take advantage of cheap water transportation, it shipped its first order for valves in July, 1901. It had been busy for several months making patterns and specialized tools under the supervision of E. P. Moorby.

While most of the shipments were made by river freight boats or by railroad, an occasional special order required "special handling." This was the situation when a 16-inch, 950-pound valve was shipped on special order via the steamboat Onteora. As the valve was being edged along that vessel's gangplank in December, 1901, a maneuver watched by many spectators at the Landing, the huge 750-pound valve unexpectedly shifted, dumping three workmen and the special order valve into the icy Hudson. Fortunately there was no loss of life.

After the completion of its two-story $12,000 brick and steel machine shop and foundry on the lot purchased from Newbury, American Valve gave employment to about 100. One tragedy marked the new building's completion when William A. Edwards fell from the roof while putting on slate; he died shortly thereafter from internal injuries. Contractor Benjamin Plusch, in May of 1907, was called upon to construct a 200-foot dock expansion to better handle the unloading of Long Island white sand for the casting process.

Enjoying a prosperity of almost two decades, including World War I, in July of 1919 American Valve began the construction of a more modern plant on the Bronk-Silvester farm near the West Shore Railroad. The foundry would continue to be a major employer for many years although at times beset with labor difficulties.

The Walter Brothers, operating under the name of The Walter Bros. Grey Iron Manufacturing, had a smaller operation at West Coxsackie producing specialty orders. The highlight of its operation was the making of a decorative iron staircase for one of New York City's famous mansions, the Joseph H. Choate residence then being erected at the corner of Broadway and Liberty Streets.

The Copper Roller-Bearing Trolley Wheel Company was enticed, in June of 1910, to remove its operation from New York City to Coxsackie, its directors at the time being Edwin H. Merriam, Edwin S. Anthony and Newton A. Calkins, all of Coxsackie, and Green B. Hamm, Jr. and William F. Wayburn of New York City. Within a few weeks of coming to Coxsackie the Board had elected Frank H. Sutherland as its president; Green B. Hamm would fill the vice president's slot. Frank F. Bedell took over the treasurer's responsibilities, assisted by Henry A. Jordan, while Edwin Anthony would serve as secretary. It is apparent these local Coxsackie men had a financial interest in the firm. Unfortunately, the trolley car for urban transportation was a dying system.

The Union Wheel and Manufacturing Company of Coxsackie was incorporated in 1919 "to manufacture, polish and buff wheels and to deal in polishers' and platers' supplies." Furnishing the necessary capital of $30,000 were six Coxsackie men: F. H. Sutherland, J. G. Newbury, W. R. Church, E. J. Miller, M. C. Richtymer and W. C. Van Alstyne. During a subsequent reorganization its name was changed to the Coxsackie Buffing Wheel Works. The largest order processed by this firm came from the Ford Motor Company when, in 1916, that corporation purchased 10,000 wheels. When the firm finally closed down, the old building on Riverside Avenue became the factory for other firms.

Although of more recent vintage, mention should be made here of related firms. The Scully Foundry was established here from Albany in 1921 as the Albrass Company. Ten years later, in 1931, an expert pattern maker and well-experienced foundry man, Leo Scully, took over the Albrass operation. The Scully firm concentrated on plumbing supplies in both wholesale quantities and in small orders. "Some were machined, pressure tested, assembled, painted, polished, packed and shipped. Steady well- known companies were customers," reported the *Coxsackie Union- News*.

State Wire and Cable originally housed at 6 River Street, former location of the Newbury Machine Shop, began operations at that site in 1944. Frank Michaelson, president, and his six workmen produced insulated wire.

The Moulding Sand Industry

The shipping of a fine grade sand, sometimes referred to as the Cadillac of that natural resource, was for many years a means of local income for laborers, businessmen and landowners. Ancient geologic activity had covered many of these flatland areas with moulding sand to a depth of a foot or more. All that was needed was to remove the layer of topsoil. In the late l9th century and into the first three decades of the 20th, many a local field and its orchard fell victim to this mining activity, both within and outside the Village limits. By heavy two-wheeled dump carts, horse and driver brought their loads to the river docks.

In the earlier years Coxsackie moulding sand moved up and down the Hudson by the bargeloads while sailing vessels of various sizes transported the cargo to east coast ports. The demand for moulding sand seemed insatiable, vital as it was to the foundries for their casting processes, a method now outmoded.

Three firms were the major Coxsackie suppliers of moulding sand. The Whitehead Bros. operated from ice house dockage above the Upper Landing; the Dolan Sand Company utilized its river front at Reeds Landing; from just above Four Mile Point, the Thomas Bell interest (later New York Sand and Facing Company) utilized its shoreline. For all three the waterways provided the cheapest means of transportation, especially for full barge or vessel loads. An occasional special order would be moved over the West Shore Railroad. In time Mike Dolan would operate from far away as the Half Moon area as local supplies of cheap sand became scarce. And water transportation was not without its risks as Thomas Bell discovered when a fast steamboat's wash upset and sunk a full bargeload off Four Mile Point, leading to a lengthy lawsuit.

Never one to do anything in a small way, Mike Dolan decided by the turn of the century to expand his wharfage to include a 10-foot high, 35-foot in depth sand shute. His dock, with its two driveways and two trap dumps, could load as much as 10,000 tons of sand in a season. This dockage right had originally been granted on June 16, 1826, to John Holton and George Beatty under State policy to promote commerce. It was now Dolan's turn to request a 120 rod grant from the Secretary of State for an extension of these "lands under water.." The Whitehead Bros. were also encouraged to rent a portion of this dockage to supplement Dolan's income.

Just above Four Mile Point, Thomas Bell had constructed a high dock on piling jutting out into the river but protected from ice floes on the north by his icehouse lands. This piling dock could accommodate two-wheeled large iron-rimmed dump carts which when driven onto a high hinged loading platform directly over a barge, could be tripped to dump and thus save hand labor.

It was not an unusual sight to see one or more sailing vessels tied up at the Dolan dock at the turn of the centruy, to take on sand cargo. Among these two-masted schooners was the Charley Woolsey of Salem, which could hold 33 tons of Whitehead Bros. sand, or the Witch Hazel of Providence.

Of these three leading sand firms, only the Whitehead Bros. survived the great depression of the 1930's, they utilizing a small sand depot at the Selkirk railroad yards for a greatly reduced volume of business.

 Newspapers

Receipts for newspaper subscriptions survive in many family archival collections; they were small printed slips of paper filled in with ink to indicate the length of the subscription and the money received. Readers at Coxsackie subscribed to a wide variety of New York and Albany publications as well as Greene County printings. Many newspapers promoted a political party viewpoint which helped insure subscriptions; others were non-partisan.

Coxsackie was not to have its own newspaper until Lawrence and Henry A. Van Dyck commenced publication of the *Greene County Advertiser*. Some historians date this paper from 1832 but a surviving printed prospectus of the Van Dycks, dated January 27, 1831, reads: "The subscribers propose to publish a Weekly Newspaper at Coxsackie to be entitled the *GREENE COUNTY ADVERTISER*. The publication will commence the ensuing Spring, early in the month of April". Unless delayed by unforeseen circumstances, this would seem to date the first Coxsackie newspaper as of the spring of 1831. Its subscription price per annum was set at $2.50 for those either calling at the office for their copies or else having carrier delivery; papers by mail were $2.00. That these Van Dycks also did job printing is indicated by surviving real property deed forms carrying their imprint.

The newspaper career of the Van Dycks was a short one, Thomas B. Carrol taking over in 1836, publishing under the masthead *The Standard*. Carrol was a very enterprising younger man, a son of West Coxsackie's wheelwright Jonathan Carrol. Within a few years Thomas B. left for more financially rewarding pastures in Albany. There, with Governor Marcy's influence, he printed many publications, and amassed a substantial competence.

Volume 1, No.1 of the *Coxsackie Union* came off the press under date of April 26, 1851, the print shop being located on the third floor of the brick building on the southeast corner of Reed and Ely Streets. Frederick W. Hoffman of Albany and his assistant, a Van Bergen, were the editors. By January, 1857, D.M. Slater and B.S. Slater were producing the issues.

After the close of the Civil War, on May 23, 1867, Charles G. Giles and William P. Franklin produced the first issue of *The Coxsackie News*; they had been publishing a weekly newspaper in central New York but were attracted to Coxsackie as a growing community. Giles terminated his interest after a few months leaving William P. Franklin as sole publisher. Later in the century his nephew, Herbert H. Franklin, would assume some responsibility. (It was this nephew, while living in Coxsackie, who experimented with and perfected an air-cooled engine which was later to be manufactured in Syracuse under the Franklin name. While at Coxsackie young Franklin also acted as agent for the Columbia bicycle.)

On March 2, 1899, the "new" *Coxsackie Union* was being distributed to readers. William P. Franklin noted in the first issue: "It was our intention to issue *The Union* two weeks ago but our material did not get here as we expected, and the railroad people broke several important parts of our big newspaper press." In that same issue Franklin advertised for local correspondents. From the start, this new *Union* series was a success, most likely due to Franklin's newspaper experience and the availability of a modern press. *The Coxsackie News* provided only modest competition. Occasionally Franklin would suborn *News* editor's work, giving credit.

The William P. Franklin editorship which had been transferred from the *News* to the *Union* came to an end with the death of the owner in January of 1921. In the settlement of Franklin's estate, the *Coxsackie News* was sold to Scott R. Hoagland, whose family were responsible for the printing of the *Oak Hill Record*. Thereafter changes came rapidly. Hoagland resold within the year to Herbert L. Rickhard, who published under the masthead — *The Union News*. Charles D. Pendell of Afton, New York, was the editor and publisher from August 1922 to September 1934 when Francis A. Hallenbeck took charge. In 1938 it was under the ownership of E. Payson and Jessamine Smith.

The concept of publishing a late afternoon daily newspaper in Coxsackie was F. Vandenbergh's; it reached readers in mid-December, 1870 under the name of *The Coxsackie Evening Herald*. At the time it was the only daily being published in Greene County. It's life was a short one.

Thomas C. Morgan (father of George T.) established *The Coxsackie Times*, a weekly Friday publication, about 1897. The next owner was publisher Pierce. The record reveals that Thomas C. Morgan and his brother sold out and went west, only to return to settle financial matters after the San Francisco earthquake. In 1906 the Morgans sold their repossessed interest in the *Coxsackie Times* (name and good will) to the *Union* publisher while the printing equipment went to Edward Silberstein for *Catskill Daily Mail* use.

A non-sectarian monthly publication of the newspaper type was published at Coxsackie in 1902 under the name of *The Christian Echo and Young People's Monthly*. The Reverend Wesley G. Price produced this sixteen-page paper. The content was dissimilar to the weekly newspapers and might more aptly be classified as a magazine. It is believed he contracted for the printing.

The Townsman was a Coxsackie Weekly which served readers from May 4, 1972 to its demise on August 14, 1975. Although it contained news articles of area current interest, it also featured historical articles and photographs from past years. "Fluffy" Ryder was a frequent contributor about river boats.

The survivor of the various Coxsackie newspapers is the *Greene County News*, printed in Catskill but maintaining a news office at West Coxsackie.

Occasionally a collector of local emphemera becomes excited by discovering an unknown Coxsackie newspaper. Actually these were special publications undertaken for specific events and were not continuing productions. A prime example is *The Still Alarm* of December, 1891, published by the Women's Auxiliary, D. M. Hamilton Engine Company No. 2, during the Coxsackie Firemen's Fair; it sold for five cents the copy. *The Still Alarm* is interesting in that it was edited by a female, Mrs. A. C. Dwight, with Miss Mamie A. Franklin serving as Business Manager.

Special Daily Extras are known to have been published at Coxsackie in 1874 during the intense excitement occasioned by the trial and murder of the county jailer by Joseph Waltz, an act which led to the calling out of the National Guard and the eventual hanging of Waltz in the old jail at the county seat.

 Shipbuilding

The earlier years of the 19th century, a time of small size yards operated by individuals or in partnership, witnessed substantial boat building activities along the Hudson. Coxsackie, New Baltimore, Athens and Catskill were such centers.

It was Dr. John Ely (Greenville) who first provided the capital and who speculated in the construction of Coxsackie sloops. About 1786 he was leasing land at Molly Wells Point (Lower Landing) "on which to build vessels." The Goodrich yard followed, its ways at various times containing the skeleton framework for sloops, barges, horse ferries and even a large steamboat hull for Roswell Reed. The location was ideal for nearness to sources of timber, skilled labor and a navigable river. Repairs to older vessels was a profitable sideline.

Coxsackie's first horse ferry, powered by horse treadmill, was a Goodrich yard product. Tunis Cochran, the master carpenter, was a versatile craftsman who could be depended upon to handle boat construction. He is known to have worked on the horse ferry in the late winter of 1819 and into the early summer months of 1820. A surviving bill for his labor to Goodrich is labeled: "For Samuel Goodrich on the horseboat."

By 1825 Samuel Goodrich, short of capital as always, appears to have persuaded Alexander Mahand to invest in the shipyard operations to the extent of financing a part of a vessel or two. It was only a temporary respite for Goodrich. On June 24, 1826, Theron Skeel, now in business at Twalfskill on Rondout Creek, instructed the law firm of Van Dyck and Bronk to arrange for the sheriff's seizure and sale of the Goodrich yard assets other than the real estate, namely "3 horses, 2 wagons, harness — one set, 2 yokes oxen, timbers in yard, 2 sleighs for wood, the Schooner Massachusetts, one half of the Sloop Ancona of Coxsackie, the New Sloop on the Stocks, and every other article which may hereafter be pointed out to him by I. and M. H. Powell." Defeated financially, Samuel Goodrich removed to Hyde Park where he attempted to reestablish himself again as a shipyard operator.

Next on the Coxsackie shipyard scene was William Mayo. Obviously a better businessman than Goodrich, Mayo operated the South River Street firm until his death. Evidence of his economic success was his impressive Greek Revival residence westerly of his shipyard (Cure's Inn in the 20th century and eventually destroyed by fire). Robert Henry Van Bergen termed Mayo "a man of remarkable pluck and enterprise."

Identified as from the Mayo shipyard are the propeller Davis (A. Davis, Stuyvesant); the Wm. Mayo (George Reed, Coxsackie); barges Harvest Queen (1857), Coxsackie (Barker and Kirtland); and the tow-boat Alfred Van Santvoord. The latter had a 90-foot keel, 21 1/2 foot beam, a 6 1/2 foot depth of hold; it was contracted for by Nelson and Company in 1853. Tunis Cochran and John Kennedy were occasional yard workers for Mayo.

Captain Wesley Hall, a veteran North (Hudson) River boatman, provided the *Saugerties Telegraph* newspaper with a series of reminiscences. His summary of the shipping history of two Coxsackie vessels is quoted:

The Wm. Mayo was built at Coxsackie in 1836 by Wm. Mayo, and she had quite a record. She was bought by Rob't. Kerr to carry stone from Wilber [Rondout Creek]. Capt. Jas. Schoonmaker took command of her. He capsized her and carried her topmast away. In about 1840 E. J. McCarthy bought her to carry stone from Saugerties. She changed captains quite frequently. Capt. Josiah Joy, David Searles, Chas. Felto, Harry Snyder, Andrew Simmons and others commanded her. Capt. Joy capsized her in a squall opposite Po'keepsie and her mast landed on the ferryboat's deck. Capt. David Searles, in a race from New London to Newport with the smart sloop Oliver Ames, and when near Point Judith carried her mast away. The Ames, after three trials, succeeded in getting a hawser to her and towed her to Newport, costing the owner, J. P. Russell, over $500. In 1868, Mr. Russell rebuilt her at an expense of $12,000. He then rigged her into a schooner and J. V. L. Crum took charge of her. A few years after Capt. Crum, when bound for Newark, she struck rock and sunk near Shooter's Island in quiet shoal water. They got her up and about 1874 J. P. Russell sold her to John Maxwell. Ezra Whitaker then took charge of her and ran her to Eastern ports with stone. In 1879, while lying at anchor in Flushing Bay in a northeast gale, she dragged her anchor and went ashore on the rocks on Riker's Island and filled with water, and in 1880, when bound down the East River, loaded with sand for the rubbing mill at Malden, he made a mistake and run her in a slip near Bridge Street, E. R. [East River] striking a ship and carried away both masts. He tore the sails into ribbons and smashed a barge's stern all in, and came very near sinking her. After that they run her as a barge until 1882 when she was sold to New Jersey parties, and is now [1900] a lighter in New York harbor.

John J. Colvin, born at Coeymans Hollow in 1815 and a long- time businessman at Coeymans, is known to have had the Oregon built by Mayo's yard. It is said it was the largest of its kind ever constructed for intended use on the Upper Hudson. Again we quote from Captain Wesley Hall:

The Oregon was built at Coxsackie in 1846 for parties in Coeymans. Her mast was 94 feet long and 28 inches in the partners. It came from the West, I think from Oregon, and cost $500. Her topmast was 66 feet. The Oregon was one of the first North River sloops that carried a long topmast and gaft topsail. About 1850 Wm. F. Russell bought her from Coeymans to carry iron from the Ulster Iron Mill. Capt. Jacob Sickles took command of her. In 1867 Capt. Jeremiah Perels bought her. He run her in the stone trade a short time, and then rigged her into a schooner and run her in the East with stone and timber. In 1874 he traded the Oregon for the propeller Blue Stone Co. with John Maxwell. Mr. Maxwell run her in the stone trade until he made the assignment in 1882. Then Capt. A. W. Hale bought her and run her to Eastern ports until 1886. He then sold her to Eastern parties to carry granite from Gloucester to Boston and vicinity. He had her about six months. In coming around Cape Cod he got caught in a gale. She could not stand the rough water and swamped, carrying one man and all the rats down with her. That was the last of the Oregon.

William Mayo operated his inn at Reeds Landing as a sideline; he also had other irons in the fire. He was the first to agitate for a local banking establishment, sought to secure a Coxsackie railroad connection, and otherwise attempted to promote Coxsackie's economic welfare.

Shortly after Mayo's death in June 1867, his widow advertised the Coxsackie shipyard and family residence for sale. The newspaper insertion reads:

Country Seat for Sale - on the bank of Hudson in the town of Coxsackie - 8 acres, fruit trees, large garden. Dwelling House - 12 large rooms - good basement and cellar finished in cement - piazza in front of house - large extension - outbuildings - ice house.

Attached to property large shipyard with all the requisite buildings and appurtenances for immediate use, including a good and valuable set of railways, with machinery and equipment complete. The above property will be sold separately or together, by applying at once on the premises to Mrs. Wm. Mayo. Coxsackie, June 13, 1867.

The $10,250 sale of the Mayo house and shipyard on South River Street was a rapid one; the purchaser in November, 1867 was John Myer of New York. Under the name of Myer, Miller & Company, the new owners soon informed the public they were prepared to "Build Vessels of All Kinds AND ALSO TO HAUL OUT REPAIR VESSELS." That they were successful in securing some business is indicated by the fact that the steamboat Jacob Leonard, built by J. E. and H. S. Baldwin at New Baltimore for the Troy Line, arrived at the Coxsackie yard in early June of 1872 where the joinerwork was to be completed.

French's *Gazetteer* (1860) was the first to note shipbuilding at Coxsackie was on the decline. This is in stark contrast to Davenport's of 1836 which stressed the fact that the yards built and repaired numerous sloops and canal boats and an occasional steamboat.

Succumbing to an offer of purchase from the Knickerbocker Ice Company in 1873, Myer sold the shipyard but with Mr. Cumming, continued to build cedar rowboats. As late as 1900 the local newspaper reported that firm was "swamped with orders."

The sloop Shakespeare had double ties to Coxsackie, it being built in the local yard and utilized for many years to haul brick of local output. When first launched in 1817, it was registered as of 99 99/100 tons burthen. Owned by Minor Hubbell, it was sold on May 17, 1843 for $225 as part of the Hubbell estate liquidation. At the time of sale, its captain was Henry Squires.

The shipbuilding effort locally reached its peak as far as size with the laying of the keel for a steamboat financed as a speculation by Roswell Reed. The Goodrich yard framed the hull mainly of cedar to prolong its life. Reed's speculation tied up most of his surplus capital; he was much relieved, according to his letters, when it was sold for approximately $7,000. The buyer, the Delaware Canal Company, instead of building the superstructure, merely roofed over the hull and utilized it to haul coal between Rondout and New York. It was registered as the Lackawanna.

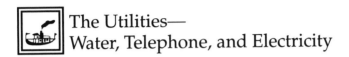

The Utilities—
Water, Telephone, and Electricity

Until the installation of indoor plumbing which greatly increased the consumption of water, many rural and semiurban households depended upon dug, stone-lined wells; natural flowing springs; streams and ponds; as well as on rainwater cisterns. The water barrel under the downspout was a boon to the weekly laundry effort, providing soft water.

As early as 1803 a proposal had been circulated to bring water from Climax to the Upper Landing, a distance of about three miles. By State Law passed April 9, 1804, Union Aqueduct Association was incorporated by Dorrance Kirtland, John Bartlett, Philip Conine Jr., Peter C. Adams, Henry Johnson, Samuel Field, Archibald McVicar, Daniel Farrey, George Wilson, Simeon Fitch, Isaac Miner Jr., Stephen Warren and John Robbins. The subscribed capital of $4,000 was used to install underground log water pipes, each approximately nine feet in length, ten inches in diameter, with a bored center hole for the water flow of two-and-a-half inches. Water did reach West Coxsackie and on to the Upper Landing where the Bakers at their trading station dealt with Hudson River sloops, the latter utilizing Climax water to fill their water butts.

The system never proved adequate for a growing village. Over the next several decades the community frequently looked to the Hudson River for a more adequate supply. The town pump at Union Square (center of merging Mansion, Ely and Reed Streets) long was a source of supply. Tenants in the corner three-story building (now State Telephone) were all pail carrying users: the newspaper on the third floor; Drs. Green & Beach, and Nathan Henry Vosburgh on the second; with Winans & Bailey, clothiers, plus Sam Marsh on the street level.

With the passage of the state law in 1889 and its subsequent amendment in 1894 authorizing villages to establish water rates and collect the same, the Coxsackie Board of Water Commissioners — T. B. Alcott (President), H. A. Jordan (Secretary), B. S. Hutchings (Treasurer), H. Van Bergen, A. Beach and D. W. Morgan — felt the need for a booklet setting forth "Rules and Regulations and Tariff of Annual Rates." It came from the *Coxsackie News* press in November, 1894, and was soon in circulation.

A permit for the supply of water into any premises required the appplicant to first state fully the several and various uses for and the manner in which the water was to be used as well as the name of the plumber employed.

Making taps and connections to the water mains ranged from $18 down to $10, depending upon the size. The booklet contained other procedures involving turning on and off water supplies, inspections of premises, etc.

Building owners were strictly forbidden to provide water to persons living in or occupying neighboring premises. The sprinkling season commenced May 1 and ended November 1, such activity being limited to a maximum of two hours daily. No party was permitted to sprinkle the street to lay the dust except in front of his own premises to the center of the street. The basic water rate was for a fifty-foot lot. Corner residents were subject to additional fees.

Water rates were payable in advance, semiannually, based upon a complicated rate of "first faucets, first tubs, first sinks, first water closets," etc. Additional faucets and fixtures came under "extra charges." Business rates varied depending upon the size of operation, the nature of the economic activity, as well as the number of faucets, wash basins, etc. Blacksmiths paid a basic rate of $5 for each "first fire" with additional hearths at $1 each. Factories, mills and shops were to be charged one rate if the labor force did not exceed ten hands for washing up purposes. Meat and fish markets, photographic galleries, drug stores, saloons and restaurants were deemed to be heavy users of water and their set rates reflected this consumption. Boarding houses had special rates depending upon whether there were more than or fewer than ten boarders. Professional offices also varied with doctors and dentists paying a higher user fee than lawyers. Depending upon the number of stalls and the washing of carriages, livery stable operators could expect to pay $2 per stall; this rate decreased to $1.50 if housing for horses exceeded eight. Recognizing that some families lived in multiple unit housing, the new schedule of rates had fees which varied for between two and four families. This was known as "shared facilities." The average householder was subject to a charge of $6 for the first faucet in the kitchen plus $1 for each additional one. The use of the boiler range for hot water cost another dollar. One wash basin in bath or sleeping room cost $1.75; one tub $3. Water closet rates depended upon the number of families using those sanitary facilities. The normal private dwelling rate for a water closet was $3. Those individuals protesting the high cost of water were privileged to request the installation of meters, provided their yearly bill exceeded six dollars. The annual Tariff of Water Rates in Coxsackie in 1894 reflects the life-style inherent in the last decade of the 19th century. Minimal sanitary facilities were the general rule, usually one bathroom and a bathtub rather than a shower. Laundry tubs rather than washing machines were the norm. Water piped to the kitchen was a necessity, constant hot water a luxury. Shared facilities in some blocks, hotels and boarding houses were far more prevalent than in today's world.

Some water system improvement came in 1880 with an expanded water distribution system and additions continued over the following years. Just before Christmas in 1894, workers and interested spectators assembled at Union Square to witness a test of "the improved water system." A stream of water, directed through hose connections, was thrown above the newspaper signal service flag staff; it was estimated this was about fifty feet above the pavement.

The *Examiner* could now report: "The Coxsackie Water Works are now completed and pronounced OK."

It was necessary to utilize the right of eminent domain to appropriate private lands for the expanding municipal water system and the Morgan dam construction in back of Roberts Hill. A three-man committee, namely C. E. Bloodgood (Catskill), Ira B. Kerr (Athens) and J. K. Hotaling (New Baltimore), was appointed to settle disputed land value claims.

By 1899 the Water Commissioner F. F. Bedell was reporting the service was being provided to 238 water takers, that 53,091 feet of water mains (various sizes) were underground and that fire protection was enhanced with 72 hydrants installed. At the December meeting of the Water Board, a yearly rate was set for each of certain commercial establishments - Cummings Hotel ($40), Eagle Hotel and barns ($42), Van Bergen Bros. Mill ($15), Miller- Hale Shirt and Collar Company ($20), and Shufelt and Titus ($20).

Though Coxsackie Villagers were confident the reservoirs and other water system improvements would meet commercial and private dwelling needs, they had not anticipated the severe drought in the summer of 1899, which cut the supply to a trickle. It was once again a choice of river water or an emergency construction effort. Against strong taxpayer opposition, the Village residents succeeded in voting approval for a bond issue at 3 1/2% in the amount of $8,500 to dam the ravine in Climax in back of the Haswell tollgate and run pipe to the Village mains. Rising to the emergency was Frank Bedell and his work crew. The voting took place on July 18 and by August 17 Coxsackie was utilizing the new water supply. In one month the men had cleared the loose rocks from around the outlet, prepared the site for the intake dam, built the dam and the pipe line.

While the public's attention was focused on this flow of water from Climax, interest surfaced on the underground route in the limestone ridge which then and still does, absorb the normal flow of water at the R. H. Van Bergen place (now Van Riper area). In early August, 1899, James G. Newbury, Arthur and Archie Newbury, William P. Franklin (newspaper editor), Charles E. Hiseerd, Bert Mann and James Murphy, all dressed in worthless old clothing, and with gas bicycle lamps, ladder and rope, descended as they later described it "Into the Bowels of the Earth."

Down the intake entrance by means of a 20-foot ladder, wrote Franklin, the group followed the stream underground about 20 feet south to an obstruction choked with driftwood. Clearing that blockage the expedition went easterly surmounting old logs, sticks and rocks some 13 feet to the top of a well made in the limestone by time, rocks and water. The well was fed by the stream's waterfall. Then lowering a 9-foot ladder the men climbed down through the fall only to find their way blocked by a pond of water of 12 feet in diameter, 30 feet in length and of an unknown depth. Using the ladder to bridge a corner of the underground pond, they crossed over into a pear-shaped passage cut about 150 feet in the solid rock. The height varied considerably but was, on the average, five feet. It tended in a southerly direction.

After traveling through this 150 foot area, they turned east down an incline to a chamber the far end of which was blocked by solid rock, thus terminating that aspect of the exploration — the stream appeared to pass under the wall, there being no visible opening. For a time the viewers' attention was focused on a large number of stalactites of carbonate of lime which were pendant from the roof. Returning, the men explored several side spur passages running in different directions. In some, logs, pieces of timber and even an old kerosene barrel were lodged firmly due to water pressure.

Recrossing the underground pond, James G. Newbury explored the pond up to his arm pits. A new lead off extended slightly upward about 35 feet to the north and at the end an "L" running 10-12 feet westerly.

The explorers having spent two-and-a-half hours in the underground passages, returned to the warm air. The disappointment, if any, came with the realization they had failed to discover any outlet.

The "Grote Fountain" which gives Fountain Flats its generic name, is another puzzlement. It falls from the limestone ridge at the base of the Thruway and thus becomes the headwater of the Coxsackie Creek. That volume of water was, at one time, utilized to power a mill. In recent years the flow has been greatly reduced.

Interest in electric power for lighting Coxsackie buildings in the Village grew rapidly after an editorial of sorts appeared in the *Coxsackie News* in September 19, 1891 carrying the headline "Give Us Light!" The immediate spur for this plea was the single electric light newly installed at the front of the Kennedy Valve Works on Mansion Street by that corporation. The more progressive residents had come to feel that the kerosene lamp had seen its day while candles were long passe. The newspaper editorial continued: "To be sure oil is cheaper than electric lights but the age is advancing and improvements are the price of prosperity."

Unlike many more urban communities who had heretofore granted franchises for the installation of mains to provide homes and businesses with gas for lighting, Coxsackie skipped from kerosene to electricity. There was a short period of time when progressive merchants installed their own systems of acetylene illuminating gas, Dayton Smith being one in his Reed Street Newsroom.

In its meeting in February, 1891, the Board of Trade considered endorsing but ended up rejecting a proposal from Daniel Kennedy, patent valve manufacturer, to supply the Village with electric lights at the rate of one dollar the month for each burner of 16 candle power, the parties using it being responsible for making the connection and paying for the fixtures; keeping them in regular repair at their own expense was an additional stipulation.

Application for an electric lighting charter was submitted to the Coxsackie Trustees as early as the summer of 1894. James G. Newbury, together with New York capital, was the catalyst. The incorporation of the Newbury interests came in 1898. Operating under the name of the Coxsackie Electric Light and Power Company, it had an initial capitalization of $20,000 which soon proved to be inadequate for a growing system. By 1899 the controlling interest in the Coxsackie Electric Light and Power Company was centered in New York at 26 Cortlandt Street, with President William A. Hengstenberg and Vice President Henry B. Newhall, Jr. making frequent quick trips to Coxsackie. The corporation sought to expand its local market with large size advertisements in the local newspapers:

> Special offer - for only one cent - Try using electricity - you can get the equivalent of 16 candles for One Hour. We give liberal discounts for quantity and early payments. Send for our information sheets. End the century by doing a good thing.

The initial street lighting, feeble as it was, brought about a demand for more. After a new and improved lamp, designated as an enclosed arc, was placed on Union Square on May 18, 1899, to enlarge the radius of light produced and prevent it from sputtering as most of the lights did, it was proposed fifteen more street lights be installed. The expansion was carried by a vote of 140 to 93, even with the opposition warning that the quarterly Village electric bill was approaching $650!

With an occasional powerhouse crisis, as when in late February of 1899 the dynamo had to be shut down due to overheating, the Village Board concluded street lighting with electricity was here to stay. Advertised for sale were the old street kerosene oil lamps; including the post, the price was set at $1.50 each. Ferry passengers had numerous compliments when a second street light was finally installed at the northeast corner of the Larabee House.

James G. Newbury had, as his goal, getting the interior of the electric light station fixed up to serve as a model operation in the state. Unfortunately, Smith Pullman upon whom the firm placed reliance, terminated his employment contract to take the position of Chief Engineer at the Hotel Kaaterskill. There were many who hoped he would return once the resort summer season was over. He had risen to the occasion when that spring had seen a heavy infestation of shad flies blamed by opponents of progress on the electric arc street lights. The dynamo brush was coated and the dynamo had to be shut down for rapid cleaning.

Improvements continued at a fast pace. Announcement of all night service to commercial establishments was an added inducement to wire the stores.

Negotiations were begun in November of 1900 to merge the Athens and Coxsackie separate electric companies and to provide a new 250 horsepower generating plant at Coxsackie. The potential for supplying the hamlet of New Baltimore was also under consideration. By late spring of 1901 the Coxsackie and Athens companies were absorbed by the Upper Hudson Light and Power Company, the necessary legal papers having been filed with the Secretary of State. The new Coxsackie station would soon be surplus property.

Telephonic communication in the Township was a fragmented operation for many years; small companies with limited capital were functioning. Long-distance service to meet the needs of businesses and professional offices, especially between Coxsackie and Albany, was the first focus of attention. Few householders were prepared to consider the private house telephone anything more than a luxury. Relatives at a distance could always be informed of deaths by the use of the telegram.

Levi Bedell was the spark plug who first rose to the challenge by raising enough capital to convince outside interests they should set the poles and string the lines to connect Coxsackie with Albany; the year was 1888. Within the next decade there was a major change in the public's attitude concerning the telephone: the home phone came to be viewed as a necessity rather than a luxury. By the year 1899 Frank F. Bedell, the entrepeneur now behind the Coxsackie Telephone Company, was ready to move. At its December 28, 1899 meeting, the Village Board, under President Arthur E. Powell, granted Bedell's request "for himself, his assigns and associates to operate and maintain a line of poles for the purpose of supporting telephone and other wires throughout the Village." The headquarters of the company, in 1901, were on the second floor of the present corner building. The public was reminded that, for their convenience, several pay telephones were available such as at O. B. Gedney's telephone, telegraph and news depot, or the James Sutherland store now occupied by Cornell Vosburgh.

Local firms were quick to size up the advantages of the telephone for enhancing retail sales, many featuring home delivery of telephone orders. Even the ferry company meeting the trains at Newton Hook advertised that as a convenience for passengers, telephone calls might be made at Mrs. Van Dyke's shoe store where they maintained a slate of notices. F. F. Bedell, with his real estate and insurance business office on the second floor of the Reed and Powell Transportation Company's block, advertised a "public telephone." The first subscriber to a telephone in Coxsackie is said to have been the insurance office of Franklin & Bedell "west of McClure's drug store."

In 1903 more long-distance poles were being installed and wires strung along the King's Road, utilizing the services of sixty workmen. "They were encamped on the Palmer Searles farm," reported the *Examiner*.

The convenience of the telephone for both emergency situations and for socializing impressed several nearby rural communities enough to form their own companies requiring a minimum of capital and equipment. The party line was an accepted situation and few, if any, viewed night service as necessary. The Ravena and Medway system was established by incorporation on April 27, 1904. The Coxsackie Flats Telephone Company was another early corporation with George Van Schaack serving as its president, Bennet C. Townsend as vice president, Myron B. Schaack keeping the secretary's books and attorney Harry McK. Curtis serving as treasurer.

In the Village, the Coxsackie Telephone Company came under the control of A. A. Gardinier, who was not very responsive to subscriber complaints about the poor quality of service. Thus it was that local stockholders turned to the State Telephone Company, which had been incorporated December 31, 1909, to operate in Ravena, Coeymans and New Baltimore. State Telephone indicated its interest in the Coxsackie operation and soon arranged for a buy-out. At the time William C. Harden was serving as president, L. A. Warren as secretary and Harry McK. Curtis as treasurer. This same company, in May of 1910, absorbed the Ravena and Medway Telephone Company. The Coxsackie Flats Company continued as a separate entity until 1946 while the line to Greenville was absorbed the previous year.

Bedell had established the Coxsackie company in space on the second floor of the present State Telephone and law office building. The State Telephone Company continued its operation from that second floor, the switchboard being located in what was to become James Warren's private law office. The building itself had been erected in the year 1853 by Roswell Reed, Jr. as a speculative investment.

BIBLIOGRAPHY

Beecher, Raymond V.: *Coxsackie Christ Episcopal Church.* Coxsackie, New
York—privately published, 1984.

Beecher, Raymond V.: *Letters From A Revolution.* Albany, NewYork, New York
State American Revolution Bicentennial Commission, 1973.

Beecher, Raymond V.: *Out to Greenville; Historical Sketches of Greene County.*
Cornwallville, New York, Hope Farm Press, 1977.

Beers' History of Greene County New York. Cornwallville, NewYork, Hope
Farm Press, reprinted 1983.

Chadwick, George H. and Vedder, Jessie V.V. (Editors): *The "OldTimes" Corner.*
Catskill, New York, Republished from The Catskill Examiner by the
Greene County Historical Society,1932.

Colles, Christopher: *A Survey Of The Roads Of The United States Of America,
1789.* Ristow, Walter W. (Editor). Cambridge, Massachusetts, The
Belkap Press of Harvard University Press, 1961.

Coxsackie St. Mary's Church: *Legacy of Faith; One Hundred Twenty-Five Years.
1854-1979.*

Coxsackie Town Bicentennial Committee: *Coxsackie On The Hudson 1776-1976,
The Hoot Of The Owl* . New Baltimore Township, Hillcrest Press,
1976.

Coxsackie Union News. Centennial Edition, April 25, 1952.

DeLisser, R. Lionel: *Picturesque Catskills, Greene County.*Cornwallville, New
York, Hope Farm Press, reprinted 1971.

Flick, Alexander C. (Editor): *History Of The State Of New York(in ten volumes).*
New York, Columbia University Press,1933.

Gallt, —: *Dear Old Greene County.* Cornwallville, New York,Hope Farm Press,
reprinted 1986.

Greene County American Revolution Bicentennial Committee, Ross,Claire L. and
Kozacek, Edward R.: *Greene County, New York -'76 Bicentennial
Overview—Beginnings and Background.* Catskill, New York, Catskill
Enterprise, 1976.

The Greene County Historical Society: *Quarterly Journals.*

Greene County Volunteer Firemen's Association: *One Hundred Years of Fire Service History—1889-1989.*

The Greene County News': *Years Ago Columns.*

Greene, Nelson: *The Valley Of The Hudson—River Of Destiny, 1609-1920 (five volumes).* Chicago, The S. J. Clarke Publishing Company, 1931.

Kenney, Alice P.: *Stubborn For Liberty; The Dutch In New York.* Syracuse, Syracuse University Press, 1975.

Kraft, Herbert C.: *The Lenape; Archaeology, History, and Ethnography.* Newark, New Jersey Historical Society, 1986.

McManus, Edgar J.: *A History of Negro Slavery in New York.* Syracuse, Syracuse University Pres, 1966.

New York State Museum Bulletin 307, January, 1936. Chadwick, George H.: *History and Value of The Name "Catskill" in Geology.*

New York State Museum Bulletin No. 332, February, 1943, Goldring, Winifred (DSc): *Geology of the Coxsackie Quadrangle, New York.*

New York State Museum and Science Service Bulletin No. 397, January, 1958, Ritchie, William A.: *An Introduction To Hudson Valley Prehistory.*

Ruttenber, E. M.: *History of the Indian Tribes of Huson's River.* Albany, New York, J. Munsell, 1872.

VanBergen, Robert H. (edited by Francis A. Hallenbeck): *Ye Olden Time as Compiled from the Coxsackie News of 1889.* Coxsackie, New York, 1935.

Vedder, Jessie Van Vechten: *History of Greene County 1651-1800.* Cornwallville, New York, Hope Farm Press reprinted 1985.

Van Der Zee, Henri and Barbara: *A Sweet And Alien Land.* The *Story of Dutch New York.* New York, The Viking Press, 1978.

Van Zandt, Roland: *Chronicles of The Hudson.* New Brunswick, Rutgers University Press, 1978.